HIS UNCONDITIONAL Love

Judy Barnes

ISBN 978-1-956696-61-5 (paperback)
ISBN 978-1-956696-62-2 (digital)

Rushmore Press LLC
1 800 460 9188
www.rushmorepress.com

Printed in the United States of America

PREFACE

HIS UNCONDITIONAL LOVE was conceived from my love of writing.

TWO GIRLS FROM NAZARETH and BORN TO BE KING were mostly fiction because not much was known about Mary, the mother of Jesus, about her birth and growing up, or about Jesus in his growing up years.

However, a lot was written about Jesus and his ministry. Consequently, I wanted to write about Jesus when he taught the people in the Holy Land.

Because so much was written about him in the Four Gospels, I decided to put another person in the story and look at things from his point of view.

I used a lot of scripture right from the New Testament from the King James Version. Sometimes the scriptural account sounded so good that I didn't think I should change the wording except when using you, your, etc. to try to make it understandable.

Hence, Benjamin was brought into the story.

I did not use the words thee, thou, thy and thine and words that may be unfamiliar to the reader. I felt the way I did it made it easier to understand.

I hope this story is interesting enough to bring new light into it.

JUDY BARNES

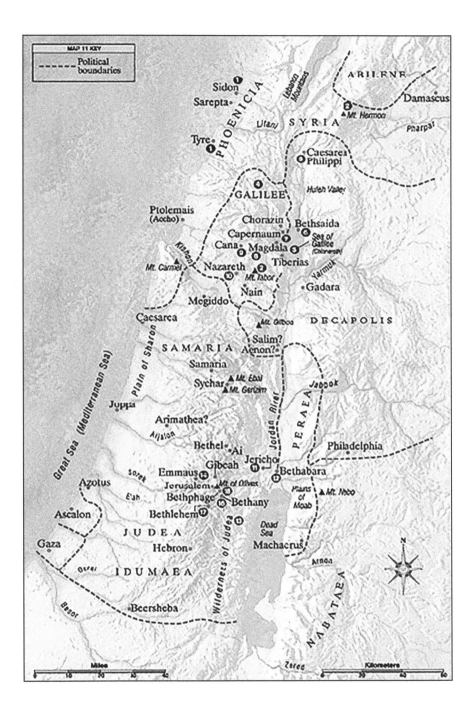

THE HOLY LAND IN NEW TESTAMENT TIME

CHAPTER
ONE

The Lonely Road

Jesus was walking along the road to Jerusalem and thinking about his family he had left behind. He would really miss his mother and brothers and sisters. They had always been a big part of his life.

Two of his brothers were working in the carpenter shop with their uncles, Aaron and Simon. Jesus knew he would not be a carpenter. He knew God had another road for him to travel. The other two brothers had decided to be fishermen and had retreated to the Sea of Galilee.

His two sisters were married and had children of their own.

Jesus was lonely and he knew he had a long way to go. He had not been to Jerusalem for a long time. He went when he was almost thirteen, but had not gone inside the Temple because he was upset because there were animal sacrifices inside and money changers selling animals for sacrifice. Instead he talked to men who were talking about points of religion.

He had gone to Jerusalem a couple of times on Holy Days before his earthly father, Joseph, was murdered.

1

He tried to teach the people of Nazareth, but they did not believe what He taught. They accused him of lying and making things up.

Everyone knew him while he was growing up and thought he was just a normal person. Why was he trying to teach them about the instructions, which he claimed he had received from God?

He decided it was time to go to Jerusalem, where hopefully, he would be able to teach the Gospel, or Good News.

While he was walking and contemplating what he would do in Jerusalem, he saw something in the road ahead. It looked like it could be a person, a man.

Was he sick? Was he drunk? Was he dead?

As he got closer he could see that the man was breathing. He was bloody and disheveled.

Jesus stopped and the man looked up at him.

The Master asked, "Are you alright? What happened?"

As he held out his hand to help the man up he said, "Who did this to you?"

The man reached for the held out hand. "Two men beat me and took all of my money."

"Would you like to come with me?"

"I would, but I am bloody and dirty. Are you sure you would want to be seen with me?"

"When we get to a stream of water, I will help clean you up", Jesus remarked.

The man beamed as this friend's invitation was extended. "Yes I would like to go with you."

"Where are we going?" The man asked.

"Jerusalem. My name is Jesus. What is yours?"

"Benjamin. I am afraid to travel by myself. You can see what happened to me while traveling alone."

It was not too long before they came to a stream. Jesus helped Benjamin clean up and he looked much better. His clothes were still soiled, but soon were better than new.

Benjamin was confused, "My clothes were bloody and dirty. Why are they now as clean as when I first put them on?"

Jesus smiled.

(Who is this man? How was he able to make my clothes as new?)

A little later, Benjamin remarked, "I am getting hungry."

Jesus confessed, "So am I."

"Go over to that fig tree and bring back some fruit."

Benjamin looked at Jesus and said, "There are no figs on the tree. It is bare."

"Look again and see."

Benjamin looked and the tree was loaded with fruit. He held his tunic up and filled it with the figs.

When Benjamin returned to Jesus there were many animals nestled around Jesus' feet.

"Where did they come from?" inquired the man.

"They came to share our meal."

There was a rabbit and Jesus stroked its fur from ears to tail. The rabbit was contented. Then a squirrel put its paws on Jesus' knee. He patted it on its head. There were also birds that nested on Jesus' shoulders. They were hungry too.

Jesus fed the animals, which would eat some of the fruit. Then he opened his hand and revealed grains and nuts for the other animals. They were all satisfied.

When the men started walking again, the animals followed close behind.

They walked all day until about sundown. It was starting to get cooler so it was decided it was time to stop. They were getting hungry again. They saw a vineyard. The grapes were ripe, so Benjamin retrieved as many as he could. They were sweet and juicy. They ate all they could and the animals ate their fill.

Jesus and Benjamin did not have anything to keep away the chill.

Benjamin said, "How are we going to stay warm. I am getting really cold. And it will be even colder during the night."

Jesus waved his hand in a circle above his head, and a warm breeze came and kept the men warm all night.

The animals had cuddled next to Jesus, and were warmed by his body.

When it was morning the men awoke as the sun was starting to warm the earth. They both stood up and stretched all of their muscles.

"Why are the animals staying with you?"

"They know that I love animals, and they will be fed as long as they are with us," Jesus commented.

Benjamin exclaimed very loudly, "I love animals too."

The birds wings started to flutter and the other animals were startled by the loud talking.

Jesus said, "We must talk in a soft voice. The animals were afraid when they heard loud speaking."

Benjamin said, almost in a whisper, "I am sorry. I will try to remember."

Jesus asked, "Where are you from? I was raised in Nazareth."

Benjamin stated, "I am from Nain. That is not too far from Nazareth. Why did you leave?"

"No Nain is not far. I was trying to teach the people and they would not believe that I received revelation from God. He tells me what to say and where I should go."

"I believe everything you tell me. I want to be with you forever."

Jesus snickered, "Forever is a long time."

Benjamin smiled, "I left Nain because nobody liked me. Everything I did was wrong in their eyes."

"Well, I guess we are lucky to have found each other. Now we both have a travel companion," Jesus related.

Again they ate grapes, and Jesus miraculously produced grains and nuts again for the ones that could not eat grapes.

Their walk began again. Soon they were greeted by a fawn, which seemed to be missing its mother.

Jesus softly petted the fawn, and it continued walking with the others. All of them got along well with each other.

Soon all of the animals dispersed and went their separate ways.

It was not very long before the men came upon two other men who seemed to be roasting a deer. Was that the mother of the fawn?

Seeing Jesus and Benjamin coming near to them, they arose from their squatting position, and charged at them.

"What are you looking at", inquired the men that were ready to eat the deer that had been roasting.

As the men were approaching Jesus and Benjamin, Jesus raised his hand and the men stopped in their tracks.

Jesus said, "We mean you no harm. We are friends."

"I do not think so", one of the men remarked. "We were going to rob and beat you, as we did the man you are standing with. I am surprised he is still alive. We gave him a good thrashing."

"Would you like to join us?" Jesus asked. "We are on our way to Jerusalem".

"Man, are you crazy? Why would we travel with you when you know our intentions?"

"As I said, we are friends."

"No," The man stated emphatically. "We will be on our way in another direction."

Jesus smiled, "Good bye, maybe we will see you again sometime."

"Not if I can help it," the man stated and the two of them ran off, leaving their roasting deer.

Benjamin and Jesus ate some of the deer and left the rest for some hungry traveler.

"How did you stop the men from hurting us," Benjamin asked.

"All I did was hold my hand up and the power of God took over."

"By the way, did I see you at the wedding in Cana?" Benjamin asked.

"I was there."

"Was it you who changed the water into wine?" Benjamin wondered.

"Yes, it was I." Jesus smiled without any explanation.

He was beginning to understand that his friend was no ordinary man.

———

The wedding at Cana is found in The New Testament John 2:1-11

CHAPTER TWO

John The Baptist

Jesus and Benjamin still had a long way to walk before they came to Jerusalem. While they walked, Jesus started telling Benjamin about the Gospel. His protégé was listening intently and trying to remember all he was being taught.

When they were coming near to Jerusalem, they saw groups of people quickly moving in a single direction.

"I wonder where they are all going. Is someone hurt or possibly dead?"

Jesus commented, "I do not know, but everyone seems to be in a hurry. I think we should follow them."

Benjamin was happy to go along with those in the group. He was getting excited.

"They are all stopping at the river. There is a man in the water yelling at the people."

When John's mother was expecting him, it was a miracle. His parents, Zacharias and Elisabeth were in their later years.

A prophet told Zacharias that Elisabeth would conceive and have a baby and that his name should be John. Zacharias did not believe the prophet, so he was struck dumb.

Three months later, in Nazareth, a young woman named Mary was betrothed to a man named Joseph. An angel came to Mary and told her that she would be the mother of the Messiah. She was a virgin and said that was impossible because she had never lain with a man. Nevertheless, she was conceived by the Holy Ghost.

Then the angel told Joseph about the miracle and he said that Mary was a virgin and had never been with a man. If she were expecting a baby, she would be stoned. She and Joseph were married right away.

The people of Nazareth said the baby was due too soon, and called her all kinds of bad names such as harlot, or prostitute.

It was decided that she would go to Jerusalem and stay with her mother's cousin, Elisabeth. That way she would be away from all the gossip. And also, she would be able to help Elisabeth before and after John was born. Joseph would go and get her after John's birth.

Joseph had to go to Bethlehem to pay taxes to Caesar Augustus. He took Mary with him. Jesus was born in Bethlehem as had been prophesized of old.

John's parents had probably died before he started baptizing the people in the Jordan River. They were elderly when he was born.

John was telling the people, "Repent for the kingdom of heaven is at hand."

John was dressed in camel's hair with a leather girdle around his waist. And he ate nothing but locusts and wild honey.

Benjamin liked the story of John the Baptist.

But when John saw many of the Pharisees and Sadducees come to his baptism, he said to them, "Oh generation of vipers, who warned you to flee from the wrath to come?"

"Show me proof of your repentance. And do not say we have Abraham for our father, for I say to you, that God can rise up children to Abraham with these stones in the river bottom."

"I indeed baptize you with water for repentance, but he that will come after me, is greater than I, whose shoes I am not worthy to bear. He will baptize you with the Holy Ghost, and with fire."

Then Jesus came to be baptized by John. But when John realized it was he, he said, "No, you should baptize me, and you come to me?"

Benjamin watched from behind some other people, wondering what his friend would do next.

Jesus said to John, "I should be baptized by you to fulfill all righteousness."

And it was done.

When Jesus came up straightway out of the water, the heavens opened, and he saw the Spirit of God descending like a dove and landing on his shoulder. And a voice from heaven said, "This is my beloved Son, in whom I am well pleased."

Next Benjamin pushed his way through the people, and stepped into the water and was baptized because he was Jesus's first disciple.

Then John went out to Jerusalem and all Judea, and the entire region around the area to baptize after they confessed their sins.

———

The story of John the Baptist is found in the New Testament Matthew 3:1-17

The story of Zacharias and Elisabeth is found in the New Testament Luke 1:1-76

The story of Mary and Joseph is found in the New Testament Luke 1:26-35

The story of Joseph paying taxes and Jesus being born in Bethlehem is found in the New Testament Luke 2:1-7

CHAPTER
THREE

Jesus's Temptation

Benjamin followed Jesus followed Jesus near to Jerusalem.

Jesus instructed his companion to stay where he was, near a log that was beside the road.

"But why am I not able to go with you?", was the question given to Jesus.

"There will be times when you cannot go where I go. This is one of those times."

Then Jesus went off by himself. He was with God, and fasted forty days and forty nights. All the while, being instructed by his Father as to what he should do and what he was to say.

All of this time Benjamin was hanging out by himself. He would leave the log long enough to hunt for some berries and edible greens. He was lonely and at night he got really cold. He had not prepared for the change of temperature between day and night.

He wondered, (Should I go and look for him? No, I was instructed to stay by this log, and that is what I will do.)

At night, he would lay by the log and cover as best he could with leaves.

When the tempter came to Jesus, he said, "If you are the Son of God, command these rocks, which are in my hand, be made into bread."

But Jesus said, "Man should not live by bread only, but by every word that comes from the mouth of God".

This was a trial to see if he would remember and do all the things he was taught by God.

Then the Devil took Jesus to the holy city (Jerusalem), and sat him on the point of the Temple. And he said to him, "Jump down. If you are the Son of God, his angels will catch you."

Jesus said, "You should not tempt the Lord your God."

Again, the Devil took him up to a very high mountain and showed him all the kingdoms of the world and the glory of them.

And he said to him, "All of these things I will give to you if you will fall down and worship me."

Then Jesus said, "Get behind me, Satan, for it is written, 'You will worship the Lord your God, and him only will you serve.'"

Then the Devil left him and the angels came and ministered to him.

———

The story about Jesus forty days and forty nights and his encounter with the Devil is found in the New Testament Matthew 4:1-11

CHAPTER FOUR

Teaching

Then Jesus returned to Benjamin. His disciple was sitting on the log. His hair and beard had gotten longer. Afterall, it had been a long wait.

Benjamin wanted to hear all of the details of Jesus's disappearance. However, he found his Master to be very quiet.

Jesus was glad to see Benjamin, but he had a lot on his mind; the forty days and nights with his Father and his encounter with the Devil, Satan himself. It had been a very exhausting episode.

Then Jesus and Benjamin walked into the city of Jerusalem and sat on a hill. The Master decided it was time to start teaching the Gospel. And Benjamin was an eager participant.

Jesus started speaking and people began to congregate to listen to the man that was sitting on a hill.

He began by saying, "Moses, our father, brought the children of Israel out of Egypt. The Israelites had been there for four hundred years.

The first while, when Joseph was alive, they were treated like royalty. After he died, the Egyptians were concerned because the Israelites were becoming more numerous and stronger. So the children of Israel were made to make bricks for the many buildings that Pharaoh wanted to build."

"The ones that were not making bricks, worked for the Egyptians in other capacities such as cooks, house cleaners, ship builders, etc. Let us put it this way, they were all slaves. Not a good position to be in."

"Moses was raised by Pharaoh's daughter, but he realized he was not an Egyptian. He started listening to the Israelites and discovered they were being mistreated."

"God told him to invoke several plagues that would distress the Egyptians. He sent frogs, lice, hail, fire, flies, locusts, and turned water into blood. But last of all he was to have the first born of everything die. The Israelites were told to paint lamb's blood on all of their door posts. And to be ready to leave as soon as they had eaten a paschal lamb."

"Pharaoh was angry. His son was one of the first born to die. He told Moses and his people to leave immediately. They did so."

"When they got to the Red Sea, Moses raised his hands and the waters divided and the people went over on dry land."

"Pharaoh, thinking he had made a mistake, sent his Army to bring them back. They tried to follow after the Israelites on dry land, but the water came behind them and they all drowned."

Benjamin's eyes were as big as saucers. He did not think he had ever heard that story before.

The crowd that had gathered was mesmerized.

Jesus continued, "The children of Israel walked for some time, until they came to Mount Sinai."

"Moses climbed the mountain and was taught by God for forty days and forty nights."

"When he came down from Mount Sinai, he carried two tablets with the Ten Commandments on them."

"While he had been gone, the people were out of control with dancing and acting the way that they should not. They also had Aaron (Moses' brother) make a golden calf to worship."

"Moses was so angry he broke the two tablets to pieces, and burned the golden calf. He put the ashes from the calf in their water and made them drink it."

After chastising the people, he returned to the mountain with two tablets he had made. He was hoping God would write the Commandments again.

"The first commandment was 'You will not have any other gods before me. That means that you should not pray to idols. Idols are made by men that do that kind of work. The idols are made like Aaron made the golden calf. They can be made in any shape and out of any material a person would want."

One man in the audience asked, "Why would anybody worship an inanimate object like that?"

Jesus answered, "Perhaps they figured God would not answer their prayers, so they went along with their neighbors who had prayed to graven images. Believe me, a graven image will not answer your prayers either."

Benjamin whispered, "What a terrible thing. I would never pray to some statue, whether two inches tall or nine feet tall. I will pray to Heavenly Father only."

"You will love the Lord your God with all your heart, and with all your soul, and with all your mind," Jesus continued.

"Do you feel you keep that Commandment?" He asked.

"I do not have a problem with that Commandment. I and my family love the Lord," one man said as he looked to his family for validation. They all nodded.

Another man stood and said, "Of course I keep that commandment."

"Where does God come in your love? Is he first in your heart and mind at all times? Does he come before your job, home and family?" Jesus asked.

The man continued, "Of course, I have to work, so I can take care of my home and family. But I pray to Him every morning, noon and night."

"What about in between? Do you think, 'What would God have me do?'", Jesus asked.

"No, I do not have time to think about Him in between," the man answered.

Benjamin felt that he understood the first commandment. God is always foremost in his and Jesus's conversation. God is most important in our lives.

Jesus felt he should continue. He had given the audience something to think about.

"Next is just as important as the first, you should love your neighbor as yourself."

Benjamin was now getting confused. "How can you love your neighbor if you do not know who your neighbor is?"

A third man rose up to speak, "I have a neighbor on one side. He is a good man from what I can tell. I never hear him talk unkindly to anyone in his family. It is easy to love him."

"The man on the other side yells a lot and I do not think he is kind to his family. I would find it hard to love him."

"We should not be respecters of people. We should not judge between the neighbors on both sides. We should love everyone unconditionally."

"Let God be the judge. It is not our responsibility to judge. God is the only true judge."

This time a woman stood up and said, "My neighbor is always borrowing something and does not ever return it. Am I supposed to love her?"

"What do you think?"

"Should I quit loaning things to her? Should I tell her I do not have that item to loan?"

Jesus said, "Should you lie?"

"No, I suppose not. What would be the right thing to do?"

"Forgive her. She is probably a good person. Maybe she just forgets to return the item. Perhaps she has a large family and she is busy taking care of them," Jesus suggested.

Then Jesus said, "You should not take the name of the Lord in vain."

"What does it mean to take the name of the Lord in vain?" Benjamin asked.

"To use the Lords name in an improper way", Jesus stated.

Jesus then continued on his sermon, "Remember the Sabbath day, to keep it holy. Six days, you should labor and do all your work. But the seventh day is the Sabbath of the Lord your God. In it, you should not do any work-you, nor your son, nor your daughter, nor your maidservant, nor your cattle, nor the stranger that is within your gates. For in six days, the Lord made heaven and earth, the sea, and all that is in them and rested the seventh day. Wherefore the Lord blessed the Sabbath day and hallowed it.

"Honor your father and your mother, that your days may be long up the land which the Lord your God gave to you."

"You should not kill."

"You should not commit adultery."

"You should not steal."

"You should not bear false witness against your neighbor."

"What does it mean to bear false witness?" Benjamin spoke up.

"That means you should not tell lies about what your neighbor says," Jesus explained

"You should not covet your neighbor's house, your neighbor's wife, nor his manservant, nor his maidservant, nor his ox, nor his ass, nor anything that is your neighbor's."

Benjamin was confused, "What does covet mean?"

"Covet means to want something that belongs to someone else," Jesus revealed.

It was starting to get dark and people started leaving to go take care of the many things that required their attention.

Jesus felt he had given everyone something to think about.

Benjamin knew his companion was tired. He had been teaching all day, without a break of any kind. So besides being tired, he was also very hungry. Benjamin knew *he* was.

He also had a question. (Should I ask him now? Or should I be quiet and let Him go to sleep?)

Jesus, feeling the dilemma Benjamin was feeling. "Do you have a question?

Benjamin just nodded.

Jesus said, "Speak on."

"We do not have a house to live in. We do not have people living on either side of us. Who is our neighbor?"

"Do we ever talk to anyone? Do I teach the people? They are all our neighbors."

"But, they do not live by us. No one does."

"No, but they are all our neighbors. Think about it; if we loved all the people we come in contact with every day, unconditionally, the world would be a wonderful place to live.""What does 'unconditionally' mean", Benjamin asked.

"That means without reservation. We love them no matter what they have done to you or to someone else. God loves all of his children. He may not love everything they do, but he still loves them."

"Does God ever cry? I mean when his children do things that are not right."

"Yes, he cries. Can you imagine being a long way from your children, but you know when they have erred? Of course he is sad, you would be too, however, you still love them."

"Ah, now I understand." Benjamin turned over and fell asleep.

Jesus and Benjamin woke up very early. There was no one to be seen.

Benjamin asked, "Why are the people not on the street by this time; we are up."

Jesus proceeded to explain what others were doing at this early hour.

"The women are getting the morning meal ready so the men and boys can be on their way to work"

"But what kind of work are the men and boys going to do?"

Jesus remarked, "There are many different types of work that they do".

"Some are fisherman, as two of my brothers are. It is hard work and very taxing. They have to make sure that the nets are mended, so there are no big holes that fish could get through. Then they have to be sure the ships are water tight. It would not do to have holes in the ships or they would sink. The boys also have to push the ships out into the water and not get wet in the process."

"Being fishermen sounds like hard work. If it should rain, they would not be able to work. I would not want to be a fisherman", Benjamin stated.

"Others go to vineyards to tend the crops. The ripe grapes have to be picked and put into pails, which then go into big vats to make into wine. That is a very productive business. They have to pick the over ripe fruit and throw those into barrels to be thrown away. Then the plants have to be weed free, which takes time. After that, the plants have to be watered and fertilized. That process usually takes all day."

Benjamin beamed, "I would like that job. I would probably be fired for eating too many grapes."

"Some tend orchards. The most popular crop is the olive. Olives are very important to the economy. The trees have to be pruned and dunged daily. The olives are picked as soon as the Master of the orchard knows they are ready. The man can tell by looking at them that they are ready, or that they need another day or so. If the trees look like they are dying, they cut some of the branches off of the good trees and graft them onto the old trees. They are very meticulous about taking good care of each tree. They do not want to lose a tree, or it will have to be cut down and put in a fire. That would mean losing the money they would make from that tree."

"I do not think that job would suit me. It sounds like backbreaking work."

Jesus smiled.

"There are people who work in the Market Place. They have to be sure and get their wares ready early for the buyers."

"The fish mongers have to be sure they are ready when the ships arrive back at shore. The fish they sell must be the freshest. By mid-day they hope to have sold most of their fish because by that time they are starting to smell bad. Usually the fish go bad at that time, because of the heat of the day."

"Bad fish smell awful. I could never be a fish monger." Benjamin said as he pinched his nose.

Jesus agreed.

"There are men who sell meat such as chickens, ducks, squab and other such meat. A woman may purchase two chickens for the evening meal. These items spoil easily, too."

"Are there any foods that do not spoil easy?"

"Not really. That is the reason people go to the market early. They want to buy the freshest food," Jesus commented.

"There are so many venders that it is hard to name them all. Apothecaries sell their pills and elixirs to people who think they have ailments, whether real or imagined.

Perfumeries are available for people to smell better. Especially harlots. It would not do for them to smell bad around their customers."

"There are men who sell animals for sacrifice for those entering the Temple. People entering that edifice are expected to buy an animal. It is easier to purchase an animal than to bring their own."

"They actually kill the animals inside the Temple?" Benjamin questioned.

Jesus answered, "Sad, but true."

Benjamin looked bewildered.

"The King's soldiers in their fine uniforms, ride around on their horses, looking for people who violate the laws", Jesus reiterated.

"They do not care for the Jews. And the Jews do not care for the soldiers. The Jews only tolerate them to keep the peace."

Benjamin said, "The uniforms make them look so official. They are beautiful."

"Yes, but you need to look at what is underneath the uniforms", Jesus exclaimed.

"The Lawyers look for people who want to sue other people for some reason, whether valid or not. That is how they earn their money."

"Sounds kind of fishy," Benjamin mused.

"And the Pharisees walk around the city with their heads held high. They try to make the citizens believe they are of high breeding. Although, if you take the clothes off, they are not any better than anyone else. They let the people think they know the law. When in actuality, they do not know much more than you or I."

"The Sadducees feel they know everything about the Mosaic Law. They teach complete freedom from the moral action and are opposed to the Pharisees belief in angels and spirits and they refuse to accept the doctrine of immortality."

"I cannot believe how much I have learned from you this morning. I am glad I am a disciple of yours," Benjamin stated.

———

The plagues of Egypt is found in the Old Testament Exodus 8, 9, 10 and 12.

The Ten Commandments is found in the Old Testament Exodus 19:16-20:21

Description of the paschal lamb is found in the Old Testament Exodus 12:5

The statements about the morning habits of the people is completely made up of my imagination

CHAPTER
FIVE

Galilee

Jesus said to Benjamin, "I feel like taking a walk. How do you feel about that?"

Benjamin beamed, "I will go anywhere with you. Where will we go?"

"We will go north to Galilee. My family is in Nazareth. I have not seen them for some time. I would like to see them and I would like you to meet them. Perhaps you would like to see your family in Nain."

Benjamin got a big grin on his face and said, "We need to get going. That is a long way."

They started walking and soon there were many people following, and along the way, more congregated. They were curious about the new principles Jesus was teaching.

As they were walking through Samaria they stopped a city called Sychar which was near to Jacob's Well.

Jesus sent all of his disciples into the city to get meat. Benjamin went with them.

Then a woman came to get water from the well.

Jesus said, "Give me some water to drink."

Then the woman said, "Why, when you are a Jew, you ask me to give you a drink? I am a woman of Samaria and Jews do not have dealings with Samaritans."

Jesus answered and said, "If you knew the gift of God, and who it is that asks for a drink, you would have asked, and he would have given you living water."

The woman said, "You have nothing to put the water in, and the well is deep. Where is the living water?"

"Are you greater than our father Jacob, who gave us the well, and drank of it himself, and his children and his cattle?" The woman asked.

Jesus answered and said, "Who drinks of this water will get thirsty again. But he who drinks of the water that I will give him will never thirst; but the water I give him will be in him a well of water springing up into everlasting life."

And the woman said, "Sir, give me this water, which I will not get thirsty, neither will I have to come here to get water."

Jesus said, "Go, call your husband, and come back."

The woman answered, "I have no husband.

Jesus said, "You have told the truth, because you have had five husbands. The one you have now is not your husband."

"I think you are a prophet. When the Messiah comes he will tell us everything."

Jesus said, "I am he you are speaking to."

His disciples came and were surprised that he would be talking to the Samaritan woman.

And many of the Samaritans of that city believed him.

He stayed two more days and taught them.

Benjamin knew in his heart that Jesus was the Messiah and a great teacher.

Jesus came into Cana of Galilee with his entourage. And there was a nobleman whose son was sick in Capernaum.

When he heard that Jesus had come to Galilee, he went to him, and begged him to come down and heal his son; for he felt that he was near death.

The nobleman said to him, "Sir, come down to my son. He is dying."

Jesus said to him, "Go, your son will not die."

The nobleman believed him and went his way.

His servants came to him and told him that his son was alive.

And he asked them the hour when the son started to heal. And they said yesterday at the seventh hour the fever left him. So the father knew that it was at the same hour Jesus told him his son lives. He and everyone in his house believed.

Jesus took his disciples and went up to a mountain. And he taught them saying, "Blessed are the poor in spirit, for theirs is the kingdom of heaven."

Benjamin questioned Jesus saying, "What does it mean to be poor in spirit?"

Jesus said, "Being poor in spirit means not prideful, but is humble. Those are the ones who will inherit the kingdom of heaven."

Benjamin remarked, "Now I understand."

Jesus continued, "Blessed are you that mourn, for you will be comforted," was the next commandment.

"Blessed are the meek, for they will inherit the earth."

Again Benjamin was confused, "Who are people that are meek? What does that mean?"

"To be meek is to be gentle and forgiving", Jesus answered.

Jesus spoke to them a parable. And he said, "A certain man had two sons. And the younger of them said to his father, 'Father, give me the portion of goods that are due to me. And he divided to him his living.'

"And not many days after, the younger son gathered everything he had together, and took his journey into a far country and there wasted what he was given in riotous living. And when he had spent all, there was a terrible famine in that land. And he wanted food and a place to live."

"And he went to a man of that country, and he sent him into his fields to feed the pigs. And he ate the husks that the pigs had. And no man would give him anything else to eat."

"And when he thought about it, he said, 'How many of his father's hired servants have enough bread and more besides? I will get up and go to my father, and will say to him, Father, I have sinned against heaven and you. I am not worthy to be called your son. Let me be a servant'".

"So he got up and came to his father. But when he was yet a great way off, his father saw him and felt sorry for him, and ran, and hugged him, and kissed him."

"And the son said, 'Father, I have sinned against heaven and you. And I am not worthy to be called your son.'"

"But the father said to his servants, 'Bring the best robe, and put it on him. And put a ring on his finger, and shoes on his feet. And also bring the fattest calf, and kill it. And we will eat and be happy. For my son was dead, and is now alive. He was lost, and he has been found.'"

"Now his elder brother was in the field. And as he came close to the house, he heard music and dancing. And he called one of the servants, and asked what these things meant."

"And the servant said, 'Your brother came home and your father has killed the fattest calf, because he has returned safely.'"

"And he was angry, and would not go into the feast."

"His father came out and asked him to come to the feast."

"And he answered his father saying, 'These many years I have served you, and I never made any trouble. And you never gave me a calf, that I might have a feast with my friends. But as soon as this son was home, which has devoured your living with harlots, you have killed for him the fattest calf.'"

"And he said to him, 'Son, you are always with me, and all that I have is yours. It is good that we should be happy and be glad. For this your brother was dead, and yet is alive. And he was lost but has been found.'"

Benjamin said, "What a wonderful story. It tells us that we should be forgiving under the worse of circumstances. That story makes me happy."

"That was the intention." Jesus smiled.

"Blessed are they who hunger and thirst after righteousness, for they will be filled."

Benjamin was excited, "I know what that means. People who want to be righteous will be righteous."

Jesus said, "You are right. Remember that."

"Blessed are the merciful for they will obtain mercy."

Benjamin asked, "Does that mean that if they show mercy to others, that God will show mercy to them?"

"You are learning", Jesus iterated.

"Blessed are the pure in heart for they will see God."

"I know", Benjamin smiled, "If you have good thoughts, then you will have a pure heart. And if you have a pure heart, you will see God in the next life."

"Right again", said the Master.

The disciples that had followed the Messiah, (besides Benjamin) were also learning what these sayings mean. They were becoming more knowledgeable with Jesus' teachings.

"Blessed are the peacemakers for they will be called the children of God."

Benjamin thought, (I want to be a peacemaker. It would be wonderful to live in a world where there is peace. And let it begin with me.)

"Blessed are they who are persecuted for righteousness sake for theirs is the kingdom of heaven."

"How can you be persecuted for righteousness sake?" Benjamin asked.

"If you are a righteous person, some men will mock you just because you are righteous," Jesus explained. "Some men are evil, and do not believe that a person can be righteous and follow God's Commandments."

"Blessed are you when men will revile you, and persecute you, and will say all manner of evil against you falsely, for my sake."

Jesus was prepared for Benjamin's question. "Reviling is the most bitter of persecution. It means to attack someone by speaking evil against them."

Benjamin could not understand why anyone would speak evil against someone because they did not like what someone said.

"Rejoice and be glad for great is your reward in heaven for the prophets were persecuted which were before you."

"I am not here to destroy the law or the prophets. I have not come to destroy but to fulfill," Jesus said.

"Who will break one of these least commandments, and teach others the same, he will be called the least in the kingdom of heaven, but those who do and teach them, the same will be called great in the kingdom of heaven."

"Agree with your adversary quickly."

Benjamin asked, "Who is your adversary?"

"The person you have an argument with is your adversary." Jesus told the people.

"Why should you agree with him? Maybe he is wrong," A man asked.

"In your eyes he may be wrong, but you should look from his point of view. Maybe you will see things differently. This person who was your adversary may turn out to be a good friend," Jesus rationalized.

Benjamin stroked his bearded chin and replied, "I see".

"You have heard, 'You should not commit adultery'. But I say to you, he that looks at a woman with lust, has already committed adultery in his heart.'"

Benjamin enquired, "What is lust?"

"Lust means that you want that woman for sexual purposes."

"Ooh, not me," Was Benjamin's come back.

"You have heard, 'An eye for an eye and a tooth for a tooth. But I say he who strikes you on the right cheek, turn to him your other cheek also."

"Ouch, why would anyone want to be struck on both cheeks? I guess that would be better than having someone pluck out your eye," Benjamin stated.

"And if a man sues you at the law, and take away your coat, give him your outer coat also."

"And if someone should compel you to go a mile, go with him two."

"Give to him that ask of you, and from him that would borrow, turn him not away."

Benjamin thought to himself (So much to remember. How will I be able to remember it all?)

"You have heard, 'love your neighbor and hate your enemy'. But I say, love your enemies, bless them who curse you, do good to them that hate you, and pray for them who despitefully use you and persecute you."

"That you may be the children of your Father which is in heaven."

"Be perfect even as you Father which is in heaven is perfect."

Benjamin said, "Perfection cannot be easy."

Jesus commented, "No, Benjamin, perfection is not easy, but it is a worthy goal."

"And when you pray, do not pray as the hypocrites do, for they love to pray standing in the synagogues and on the street corners so people will see them. I say, they have their reward. However, when you pray, enter into your secret place and shut the door. Pray to your Father which is in secret, and your Father which sees you in secret will reward you openly."

"When you pray, do not use vain repetitions as the heathen do, for they think that they will be heard for their much speaking. Your Father knows what you need before you ask him."

"You should pray like this: Our Father which is in heaven, Hallowed be your name. Your kingdom come, your will be done in earth, as it is in heaven. Give us today our daily bread. And forgive us our debts, as we forgive our debtors. And lead us not into temptation, but deliver us from evil: For yours is the kingdom, and the power, and the glory forever."

"For if you forgive men their trespasses, your heavenly Father will also forgive you. But if you do not forgive men their trespasses, neither will your Father forgive your trespasses."

"Lay not up for yourselves treasures on earth, where moth and rust can corrupt them, and where thieves can steal: But lay up for yourselves treasures in heaven, where neither moth nor rust will corrupt them, and where thieves do not steal. For where your treasure is, there will your heart also be."

Benjamin thought, (So so much to digest in one sitting.)

———

Teaching the Samaritan woman is found in the New Testament John 4:4-43

The nobleman's son was sick at Capernaum is found in the New Testament John 4:46-53

The Beatitudes are found in the New Testament Matthew 5:3-6:21

The parable of the Prodigal Son is found in the New Testament Luke 15:11-32

Naming The Twelve Apostles

While Jesus was in the mountain with his disciples, he prayed to his Father all night.

When it was day he called his disciples and of them he chose twelve.

Benjamin was there also, and he wondered if he would be called to be one of his apostles.

Simon, who Jesus named Peter, and Andrew his brother, and James and John, Philip and Bartholomew.

Benjamin thought, (I must be next. Jesus would not forget me.)

Matthew and Thomas, James the son of Alphaeus, and Simon called Zelotes, and Judas, the Brother of James, and Judas Iscariot.

Benjamin said, "Master, what about me? I have been with you from the beginning. Can I be an apostle also?"

"Yes, Benjamin you have been with me for a long time. You are my friend and disciple."

"The twelve I will send out to teach the people. You will stay with me and continue to be my disciple and my friend."

And he came down from the mountain: his disciples, apostles, and his friends. There was a great multitude of people from Judea and Jerusalem, from the sea coast of Tyre and Sidon, who all came to hear him. And he healed their diseases.

And they all walked again. Benjamin wondered, (When will I be able to meet his mother and brothers and sisters?) He continued to walk with Jesus.

And they went to Capernaum on the Sabbath and taught in the Synagogue. And there was in their Synagogue a man with an unclean spirit. And he cried out in a loud voice saying, "Let us alone, what have we to do with you, Jesus of Nazareth? Did you come to destroy us? I know who you are, the Holy One of God."

And Jesus said, "Be quiet and come out of him."

When the evil spirit had torn him, and cried with a loud voice, he came out of him.

And they were all amazed, and they questioned among themselves, saying, "What is this, what new doctrine is this? For with authority he commands the unclean spirits, and they obey him."

When they came out of the Synagogue, they entered into the house of Simon and Andrew with James and John. Benjamin and the other disciples stayed outside.

Simon's wife's mother lay sick with a fever and they told him right away.

And Jesus came and took her by the hand and lifted her up, and immediately the fever was gone.

When the sun set, the people brought all the sick and those who had devils in them and he healed them.

Benjamin thought, (Jesus must be getting tired. He has been teaching and preaching all day long.)

His followers stayed close to him, so he decided to go to Lake Gennesaret and he saw two ships, but the men were not in them, they were cleaning their nets.

He stepped into one of the ships, the one belonging to Simon and asked him to push the ship a little way off the shore. And he sat down and taught the people from the ship.

When he had finished speaking he asked Simon to launch him into the deep water, and let down the net.

Simon said, "Master, we have been fishing all night and have nothing. But at your word we will let them down again.

Then they enclosed a great amount of fish and the net broke. Then Simon Peter called to his partners which were in the other ship to come and help him.

They came and helped him and they caught so many fish that the ships began to sink.

When Simon Peter saw it, he fell down at Jesus' knees saying, "Depart from me, for I am a sinful man, O Lord", for he was astonished because of the amount of fish they had taken.

Benjamin also was amazed at the amount of fish. He knew he should not be astonished: Afterall, Jesus is the Messiah.

A man with Leprosy came to Jesus later and worshipped him and said, "If you will, you can make me clean."

And Jesus put his hand on his head saying, "I will. Be clean."

And immediately his leprosy was cleansed.

"Do not tell any man, but go to the priest and give him a gift that Moses commanded as a testimony to them", Jesus told the man.

———

The Twelve Apostles named is found in New Testament Luke 6:14-16

Jesus Drives an Evil Spirit from a man in Capernaum is found in the New Testament Mark 1:21-27

Jesus Heals Peter's Mother-in-Law Sick with Fever is found in the New Testament Matthew 8:14-15

First miraculous Catch of Fish on Lake Gennesaret is found in the New Testament Luke 5:1-11

Jesus Cleanses a Man With Leprosy is found in the New Testament Matthew 8:2-4

Jesus Heals a Centurion's Servant with Palsy at Capernaum is found in the New Testament Matthew 8:5-13

CHAPTER
SEVEN

Galilee

(CONTINUED)

Jesus, Benjamin and his apostles, decided to stay in Galilee. He still had not seen his family.

While he was on his way to Nazareth he stopped in the city of Nain. And, of course, Benjamin, his apostles, and many others followed him. And that was where Benjamin was raised.

When he came to the gate of the city, there was a dead man carried out, the only son of his mother. And she was a widow and there were a lot of people of the city were with her.

And when Jesus saw her, he felt sorry for her and said, "Do not cry."

And he came and touched the bier. Those who carried it stood still.

And he said, "Young man, I say arise."

He that was dead, sat up and began speaking. And Jesus delivered him to his mother.

And many were afraid, however, they glorified God, saying, "A great prophet is here among us. God has visited his people."

John the Baptist called for two of his disciples and sent them to Jesus saying, "Are you the one that should come?" Or should we look for someone else?"

And in that same hour Jesus cured many of their afflictions, plagues; and to many that were blind, he restored their sight.

Then Jesus answered, "Go and tell John the things you have seen and heard. How the blind see, the lame walk, the lepers are cleansed, the deaf hear, the dead are raised, and to the poor the gospel is preached."

"What did you go to see? A prophet? Yes and he is much more than a prophet."

"Among those that are born of women there is not a greater prophet than John the Baptist."

Benjamin was anxious to see his family. However, they would not receive him.

His brother said, "Send him away. He keeps company with Jesus who is a liar and blasphemer."

Benjamin was sad, but he was glad he was a good friend of Jesus, the Messiah.

Jesus, and those who followed, continued on their way to Nazareth.

When they came to Mary's house she came out to meet them.

Benjamin remarked, "Why is that big rock in front of the house?"

Jesus smiled. There are a lot of good memories associated with that protrusion.

"The stories that go with that rock are complicated", Jesus answered.

"A long time ago, before my mother was born, the rock was here. There was nothing around it. My mother and her friend Mary Elizabeth used to play there. They started out playing with their dolls. They would pretend to be mothers and take care of their pretend babies. Later, as they were growing up, they would pretend they were princesses waiting for their handsome princes on camelback to marry them and take them away to some exotic country. Also, they used the rock to get together and tell secrets. When we moved from Egypt back to Nazareth, I was five years old. I wanted to sit on the rock. I continued to sit on it until I left Nazareth and came to Jerusalem."

"That is a long story. Why was your mother's house built right by the rock", Benjamin asked.

"My earthly father thought that would be a wonderful betrothal present."

Benjamin commented, "I agree. That was a fantastic present."

"I think we should go to the carpenter shop and meet my brothers and uncles."

Benjamin agreed. He followed Jesus to meet part of his family. Of course, the whole entourage were close behind.

When Jesus opened the door, he was immediately greeted with hugs.

"This is my uncle Simon and my other uncle Aaron." They nodded and smiled to everyone. The people outside reciprocated with nods and smiles.

Next he introduced two of his brothers who also were carpenters. "This is my brother Simon and the other one is Judas." They also nodded and smiled at the group.

And the people were thrilled to meet Jesus' brothers.

They only stayed a few minutes and were anxious to meet his wonderful mother.

Benjamin was so excited to meet Mary, he could hardly stand it.

They all walked to the house by the huge rock. Mary saw them coming and went outside to greet them. She invited Jesus, Benjamin and the twelve into the house. There just was not enough room for everybody. She thought it was wonderful that so many people followed her son. He did not have that kind of reception when he lived in Nazareth.

She was so proud of Jesus. She knew he was a teacher, but she did not know to what extent he taught and where he received his information.

She should have known where he received his information. She knew from the beginning that he was the Son of God. Therefore, where would he receive his knowledge and information, but from God himself?

Mary pulled Jesus aside and revealed to him that she was not able to feed such a large group.

Jesus said, "Do not worry about it. You fix what you can and believe me, they will all be fed and filled."

Mary was pessimistic, but trusted in her son.

She had some lamb and vegetables and some fruit. She looked at it pathetically. (How was this going to be accomplished?)

Mary fixed the scanty amount of food that she had. And the people walked in and prepared their bowls and retreated outside to devour the succulent delight.

Benjamin could not believe that all of the people were fed. The food was delicious. Mary was amazing! There must have been nearly one hundred followers that were fed and filled.

Jesus read Benjamin's thought and had to agree that his mother is amazing.

Mary asked, "Has everyone had enough?" She looked around to see if any were lacking.

Then she continued, "My wonderful son, Jesus, provided the excess. Please thank him. I contributed what I had, which was not very much. However, you are all filled."

Benjamin conceded the fact that his friend had miraculously provided the dinner.

Everyone, with their belly's full lay outside and slept. Jesus, Benjamin and the Twelve slept on the floor inside the house.

The ones outside stayed alert, so they could assert the movement of Jesus. When he was ready to leave, they also wanted to be ready. They did not want to miss anything that he should do.

About sunup, Jesus was up. He woke his disciples and departed out the door, after giving his family big hugs.

Mary made the statement, "I will be coming to Jerusalem soon to be with you. I know some of your brothers will go with me."

Everyone walked all day and when evening came they were by the Sea of Galilee.

Jesus and his disciples, and of course Benjamin, climbed into a ship and proceeded to go to the other side.

Unfortunately, a boisterous storm arose. Jesus and Benjamin were sleeping.

The waves were coming over the ship and his disciples thought the ship would sink.

His disciples woke him, saying, "Lord, save us; the ship is sinking and we will all drown."

Benjamin woke up, also, and rubbed his eyes, wondering what all of the commotion was about. When he realized what was happening with the storm, he panicked. "Save us, Master. Otherwise we will perish."

Then Jesus said to them, "Why are you afraid? Oh you who have lost your faith."

So he arose and ordered the wind and the sea to be calm.

Benjamin stayed calm. He knew Jesus would be able to do whatever was necessary to make sure all would be safe.

But the other men marveled, saying, "What kind of man is this, that even the winds and the sea obey him."

By this time, they should have known, Jesus could do all things.

And when he had come to the other side of the Sea of Galilee into the country of the Gergesenes, two men possessed with devils, were coming out of the tombs. They were exceedingly mean and would not let anyone go in that direction.

And, they cried out, "We do not have anything to do with you, Jesus, Son of God. Do you come this way to torment us?"

When Jesus looked a good way off and saw a herd of pigs eating.

So the devils said to him, "If you cast us out, make us go away into that herd of pigs."

And he said to them, "Go".

And when the devils came out of the men, they went into the herd of pigs. And the whole herd ran violently down a steep hill into the sea, and they drowned.

And the men that were in charge of the pigs ran away and went into the city and told everyone what Jesus had done to the men that were possessed with the devils.

———

Jesus saves widow's son is found in the New Testament Luke 7:11-17

John, the Baptist asks if it is he that should come is found in the New Testament Luke7:18-28

Jesus calms the storm is found in the New Testament Matthew 8:23-26

Jesus casts Demons into the herd of pigs is found in the New Testament Matthew 8:28-33

CHAPTER EIGHT

Judea and Parables

Jesus decided it was time to leave Galilee and return to Judea. He started walking again and went south.

All of his disciples and friends followed close behind him.

After these things the Lord appointed seventy also, and sent them two and two before he would go there.

Then he said to them, "The harvest truly is great, but the laborers are few."

"Go your way, behold, I send you as lambs among wolves."

"And when you enter in a house, first say, 'Peace be to this house.'" "He that hears you, hears me, and he that despise you will despise me, and he that despises me, despises him that sent me."

And the seventy returned again with joy, saying, "Lord, even the devils are subject to us through your name."

And he said to them, I saw Satan as lightning fall from heaven."

And he turned to his disciples, and said privately, "Blessed are the eyes which see the things you see."

And a lawyer asked, "Who is my neighbor?"

Jesus answering said, "A certain man went down from Jerusalem to Jericho, and fell among thieves, which stripped him and wounded him and left, leaving him half dead."

"And by chance a priest came that way, and when he saw him, he passed on the other side."

"Likewise, a Levite, when he came and looked at him, and passed on the other side."

"But a certain Samaritan, as he journeyed, came where he was, and when he saw him, he felt sorry for him. He went to him and bound up his wounds, pouring in oil and wine, and set him on his own beast, and took him to an Inn, and took care of him."

"And on the morrow, when he left, he took out some money, and gave it to the host, and said to him, "Take care of him, and whatsoever more that you spend, when I come again, I will repay you."

"Now which of these three, do you think, was the neighbor to him that fell among thieves?"

And he said, "He that showed mercy on him."

Then Jesus said, "Go and do the same."

Now it came to pass, as they went, that he entered into a certain village called Bethany.

And a certain woman named Martha took him into her house.

And she had a sister called Mary, which also sat at Jesus' feet, and heard his word.

But Martha was busy getting ready to serve him, but came to him, and said, "Lord, do you not care that my sister has left me to serve alone? Tell her to help me."

And Jesus answered, "Martha, Martha, you are worried about many things, but one thing is needed, and Mary has chosen that good part, which will not be taken away from her.

Jesus sat by the sea side.

And very many followers gathered together to hear him. He went into a ship and sat. And all of the people stood on the shore.

And he spoke many things to them in parables, saying, "A sower went in his field to sow seeds."

"Some fell on stony places, where there was not much soil. And they grew because they had no deepness of soil."

"And when the sun came up, they were scorched. And because they had no root, they withered away."

"And some fell among thorns. And the thorns grew up, they choked them."

"But others fell in good soil, and brought forth fruit, some a hundred fold, and some sixty fold, and some thirty fold."

"Who has ears to hear, let him hear."

Benjamin came to Jesus and said, "Why do you teach the people in parables?"

He answered and said, "Because you know the mysteries of the kingdom of heaven, but to them it is not given."

"For whosoever has, to him will be given, and he will have much more. But whosoever has not, from him will be taken away even what he has."

"Therefore, I speak to them in parables because they seeing see not, and hearing, they hear not, neither do they understand."

"And in them the prophecy of Esaias is fulfilled, which says, 'By hearing you will hear, and will not understand, and seeing you will see, and you still will not understand.'"

"For the people's heart is waxed gross, and their ears are dull of hearing, and their eyes have closed. Because if at any time they should see with their eyes, and hear with their ears, and will understand with their heart, and should be converted, and I should heal them."

"But blessed are your eyes, for they see, and your ears, for they hear."

"For I say to you, that many prophets and righteous men have desired to see those things which you see, and have not seen them, and to hear those things which you hear, and have not heard them."

Benjamin listened intently, so that he will be able to understand the parables. For they are a mystery to him. But if he hears them enough, hopefully, he will start to see and hear the parables that Jesus teaches.

As he listened, Jesus began to explain the meaning of the sower.

"When anyone hears the word of the kingdom, and does not understand it, then comes the wicked one, and takes away that which was sown in his heart. This is he which received the seed by the way side."

Benjamin smiled, (Now, I understand. Satan takes the things away that the Sower has put into the heart of man that did not grow because it was not put into his heart because he did not understand that he was not ready to hear the truth.)

"He that received the seed in stony places, the same is he that hears the word, and not with joy receives it."

(A man hears the word, but he rejects it because he did not receive it with joy.) Benjamin mused about that part.

"Yet he has not root in himself, but listens for a while. However, when tribulation or persecution comes, because of the word, he is offended."

(Yes, he has not been converted, so when trials come, he no longer believes. I'm sure I understand that one.)

"And he that received the seed among the thorns is he that hears the word, and the care of this world, and the deceitfulness of riches, choke the word, and he becomes unfruitful."

(That man hears the word but does not believe it because of lies and his riches are more important to him. But he will not receive the riches in heaven.)

"But he that received seed in the good ground is he that hears the word, and understand it, which also brings forth fruit."

(He hears the word of God and understands it and has place in the kingdom of heaven.)

"Another parable he told to them, saying, 'The kingdom of heaven is like a man which sowed good seed in his field."

"But while men slept, his enemy came and planted thorns among the wheat, and went away."

"When the wheat grew, and brought forth fruit, then came the thorns also."

"So the servants of the householder came and said to him, 'Sir, did you sow good seed in your field? Why is there then thorns?'"

"He said to them, 'An enemy has done this.' The servants said to him, 'Would you like us to go and gather them?'"

"But he said, 'No, unless while you gather the thorns, you root up the wheat with them.'"

"Let both grow together until the harvest. And in the time of harvest I will say to the reapers, 'Gather together first the thorns, and bind them in bundles to burn them, but gather the wheat and put it in my barn.'"

Benjamin understood that parable. That was an easy one.

Jesus told them another one. "The kingdom of heaven is like a grain of mustard seed, which a man took and sowed in his field. Which indeed is the least of all seeds. But when it is grown, it is the greatest among herbs, and becomes a tree, so that the birds of the air come and live in the branches.

Then Jesus sent the multitude away, and went into a house. And his disciples, including Benjamin, came to him saying, "Tell us the meaning of the thorns of the field."

He answered and said to them, "He that sows the good seed is the Son of man."

"The field is the world. The good seed are the children of the kingdom. But the thorns are the children of the wicked one."

"The enemy that sowed the thorns is the devil. The harvest is the end of the world, and the reapers are the angels."

"As the thorns are gathered and burned in the fire, so will it be in the end of the world."

"The Son of man will send his angels, and they will gather out of his kingdom all things that offend, and them which do iniquity. And will cast them into a furnace of fire, and there will be wailing and gnashing of teeth."

"Then will the righteous shine forth as the sun in the kingdom of their Father."

"Who has ears to hear, let him hear."

"Again, the kingdom of heaven is like a treasure hid in a field, which when a man has found, he hides it. And for joy, goes and sells all he has, and buys that field."

"Again, the kingdom of heaven is like a merchant man, seeking goodly pearls, who when he found one pearl of great price, went and sold all that he had, and bought it.

"Again, the kingdom of heaven is like a net, which was cast into the sea, and gathered of every kind. Which, when it was full, they drew to shore, and sat down, and gathered the good into vessels, but cast the bad away."

"So it will be at the end of the world. The angels will come and sever the wicked from among the just, and will cast the wicked into the fire. There will be wailing and gnashing of teeth."

Jesus then said to them, "Have you understood all these things?"

They said to him, "Yes Lord."

And it came to pass, that when Jesus had finished these parables, he departed.

And when he came to his own country, he taught them in their synagogue.

They were astonished, and said, "When has this man gained his wisdom and his mighty works."

"Is this the carpenter's son? Is not his mother called Mary? And his brothers, James, and Joses, and Simon, and Judas? And his sisters, are they also with us? Why then does this man knows all these things?"

And they were offended by him. But Jesus said to them, "A prophet is not without honor, except in his own country, and in his own house." And he did not do many mighty works because of their unbelief."

There was a man of the Pharisees, named Nicodemus, a ruler of the Jews.

He came to Jesus at night, and said to him, "Rabbi, we know that you are a teacher who has come from God. For no man can do these miracles except that God be with him."

Jesus answered him saying, "I say to you, except a man be born of water and of the spirit, he cannot enter into the kingdom of God."

"That which is born of the flesh is flesh; and that which is born of the Spirit is spirit."

"Marvel not that I said to you, you must be born again."

"The wind blows where it wants, and you hear the sound of the wind, but cannot tell where it comes from or where it will go. So is everyone that is born of the Spirit."

Nicodemus answered and said, "How can these things be?"

Jesus said to him, "You are a master of Israel, and do not know these things?"

"I say to you, we speak of what we know, and testify what we have seen. And you do not receive our witness."

"If I have told you of earthly things, and you do believe, how will you believe, if I tell you of heavenly things?"

"And no man has ascended up to heaven but he that came down from heaven, even the Son of man which is in heaven."

"For God so loved the world, which he gave his only begotten Son, that whosoever believes in him will not perish, but have everlasting life."

"For God sent not his Son into the world to condemn the world; but that the world through him might be saved."

He and all of his followers went into Jerusalem because he said, "I will try and teach the citizens the things I was able to teach the people of Galilee.

Benjamin was glad to be back to Jerusalem. He felt more comfortable there, although the Pharisees and Sadducees were always trying to catch Jesus in a snare.

They felt the things he was teaching was blasphemy and things he was making up as he went along.

As Jesus went to all of the cities and villages, he was teaching in their synagogues, and preaching the gospel of the kingdom, and healing every sickness and every disease that the people had.

While he was teaching, a woman, had had an issue of blood for twelve years. She had suffered many things of many physicians, and had spent all that she had, and was not healed, and it kept getting worse.

She had heard of Jesus, and came in the crowd behind him and touched his clothing.

Because she said, "If I may just touch his clothes, I will be healed." And right away she felt better. Her issue of blood dried up, and she felt in her body that the plague was gone from her.

And Jesus felt that someone had touched him and he said, "Who touched my clothes?"

Benjamin said, "Look at all the people. Many have touched you. How is it that you could feel one special person that touched your clothes?"

Jesus turned around and looked at the woman who had touched his clothes.

But the woman was afraid and trembled, knowing what was done in her. She fell down before him, and told him the truth.

And he said to her, "Daughter your faith has healed you. Go in peace, and be healed of your plague."

There came a man named Jarius, and he was a ruler of the synagogue. And he fell down at Jesus' feet, and begged him to come to his house. For he had one daughter, about twelve years of age, and she lay dying. But as he went the people crowded around him.

Then one came from the ruler of the synagogue's house and said, "Your daughter is dead, do not trouble the Master."

But when Jesus heard it, he said to him, "Be not afraid and believe only, and she will be healed."

And when Jesus came to the house, he did not want any man to go in with him except Peter, James, and John and the father and mother of the girl.

Benjamin wondered why he was not one to watch what was going on. He and Jesus were still close friends. A sadness came over him.

The mourners were not in the room with the girl, but they wept and mourned for her, and Jesus said, "She is not dead, but sleeps."

And they laughed because they knew she was dead. He sent them all out of the house, and called, saying, "Maid arise."

And her spirit came again, and she arose and he commanded them to give her food.

And her parents were astonished but he told them to tell no one what was done.

Even though, Benjamin had seen so many miracles done by Jesus, he was still amazed when he saw someone else healed. And he still liked to watch when a miracle took place.

He knew the miracles were done by the power of God, but he was still in awe. A lot had happened since the long walk to Jerusalem. That was just Jesus, he and some animals. How he missed those times alone with his best friend. Now there was a multitude of people around him all the time.

"I doubt if we will ever have time alone together. Just the two of us, and maybe a few animals."

When Jesus came out, Benjamin asked, "Why was not I allowed to be with you when you healed the girl?"

Jesus took him aside and explained, "Peter, James and John needed to be with me to learn how the miracle was accomplished. Then they will be able to do the same things when I am no longer with them."

Benjamin asked, "Lord, where are you going?"

"I will go to be with my Father."

"Can I go with you?" he wondered.

"No one can go with me. I will have completed my time on earth."

Benjamin thought he understood, but he was not happy about it.

When Jesus and all of his companions (approximately two hundred), started walking again, two blind men followed him whining and crying saying, "Son of David, have mercy on us."

When he came to the house he was walking to, he went inside and the men followed him in. Then Jesus said to them, "Do you believe that I can heal both of you?"

And they said, "Yes, Lord".

He then touched their eyes, saying, "According to your faith, be healed."

And their eyes were opened and Jesus said to them, "Do not tell anyone what has been done to you."

But when they left him, they told everyone they came in contact with. His fame was spread all over the country.

As they were again walking, his disciples brought to him a dumb man possessed with a devil.

And when the devil was cast out, the man spoke and the followers were astonished and said, "It was never before seen as this was done in all Israel."

But the Pharisees said, "He casts out devils through the prince of devils."

They meant that Jesus was not able to cast out the devil except he himself was a devil.

———

Jesus teaches Nicodemus about being born again is found in the New Testament John 3:1-17

Woman Healed of an Issue of blood is found in the New Testament Mark 5:25-34

Jesus raises Jarius Daughter Back to Life is found in the New Testament Luke 8:40-42 and 49-56

Jesus Heals Two Blind Men is found in the New Testament Matthew 9:27-31

Jesus Heals a Man Who Was Unable to Speak is found in the New Testament Mathew 9:32-34

Jesus instructs the seventy is found in the New Testament Luke 10:1-20

Who is my neighbor is found in the New Testament Luke 10:25-37

Parable of The Good Samaritan is found in the New Testament Luke 10:30-35

Parable of The Sower is found in the New Testament Luke 13:3-9

Reasons for Parables is found in the New Testament Luke 13:10-17

Meaning of the Sower is found in the New Testament Luke 13:18-23

Parable of the Kingdom of Heaven is found in the New Testament Luke 13:24-30

Parable of The Mustard Seed is found in the New Testament Luke 13:31-32

Parable of the Thorns is found in the New Testament Luke 13:36-43

Parable of the Treasure is found in the New Testament Luke 13:44

Parable of the Pearl of Great Price is found in the New Testament Luke 13:45-46

Parable of the fish is found in the New Testament Luke 13:47-52

Explanation of Jesus' Brothers and Sisters is found in the New Testament
Luke 13:53-58

CHAPTER
NINE

More Miracles

"Walking, walking, it seems like all we do", Benjamin complained.

Jesus talked to him and said, "I know we walk a lot, but we must do that to reach all of the people who need help."

"I know. I am sorry I complained. I love being with you and the apostles and watching you perform miracles. I did not know that anyone could do the things you do".

Jesus understood the way Benjamin felt. There were times when he did not think he could go any further.

"Benjamin, we are going back to Galilee. They are receptive to the things I teach. Besides the Pharisees do not try to catch me in their snares."

Benjamin really did not care where his friend went as long as he could go too. Even though he was not an apostle, he knew Jesus would always want him around. And he treated Benjamin as well as he treated the twelve. He felt like he was the thirteenth apostle.

(Off we go to Galilee.)

It was wonderful having Mary and James and Joses walking with them. They were able to witness the miracles Jesus performed. Mary was proud of all of her sons, but she always knew from the beginning of her inception that Jesus would always be special to the whole world. That fact was being realized every day. She was glad that she was able to be with him almost all the time now.

When they came to Nazareth, Mary stopped long enough to make sure everything was being handled by her other sons Simon, named for his uncle, and Judas.

Aaron and the elder Simon were still there, but would soon be retiring because they were quite old.

When everything checked out perfect, they all were ready to walk again.

All of a sudden, Jesus turned himself around and started heading in the way they had just come.

Benjamin asked, "Where are we going? I thought you had teaching you wanted to do in Galilee. We seem to be heading back toward Jerusalem."

"Yes, I feel there is more to be done there before we come again to Galilee."

No more needed to be said.

The walk seemed long and tedious. Jesus was tired, as were his apostles and disciples.

By this time there were about five hundred followers. No one wanted to miss anything that would happen.

Soon after they returned to Jerusalem there was a feast of the Jews, and Jesus went to it.

There is at Jerusalem by the sheep market a pool, which is called Bethesda, which had five porches.

There lay a multitude of people who had many afflictions, waiting for the moving of the water. For an angel went down at a certain season into the pool, and moved the water. Then the first person who would step into the water was healed of whatever disease he had.

And a certain man was there, which had had a disease thirty-eight years.

When Jesus saw him lie, and knew that he had been there a long time. He said to him, "Would you like to be healed?"

"Sir, I have no man, when the water is moving, to put me into the pool."

Then Jesus said, "Rise, take up your bed, and walk."

And immediately the man was healed, and it was the Sabbath day.

The Jews said to him that was cured, "It is the Sabbath day. It is not lawful for you to carry your bed."

He answered them, "He that cured me, the same said to me 'Take up your bed and walk.'"

"What man is it which said to you, 'Take up your bed and walk?'"

"Do you not know who it was?" The healed man asked. "For Jesus had vanished, because of the multitude being in that place."

Afterward Jesus saw the man in the temple, and said to him, "You are the man who was healed. Sin no more, or a worse thing will come to you."

The man left, and told the Jews that it was Jesus which had healed him.

After these things came Jesus and his disciples into the land of Judea; and there he stayed with them and baptized many people.

And John the Baptist was also baptizing near Salim, because there was a lot of water there. And many came and were baptized. For John was not yet in prison.

Jesus sent the twelve out two by two to preach the gospel that men should repent. And they cast out many devils, and anointed with oil many that were sick, and healed them.

And King Herod heard of him and he said John the Baptist had risen from the dead, and mighty works do show themselves in him.

Others said it was Elias. And others said that it is a prophet, or one of the prophets.

But when Herod heard of it he said, "It is John, whom I beheaded. He is risen from the dead."

For Herod, himself had sent for John, and bound him in prison for Herodias' sake, his brother Philip's wife. For he had married her.

For John had said to Herod, "It is not lawful for you to have your brother's wife.

Therefore, Herodias was angry with John and would have killed him, but she could not.

Herod was afraid of John because he knew he was a good man.

When it was Herod's birthday, he made a supper for his lords, high captains, and the chiefs of Galilee.

And when the daughter of Herodias came in, and danced, and pleased Herod and them that sat with him, the king said to the damsel, "Ask me what you will, and I will give it to you."

And she went to her mother and said, "What should I ask?"

And Herodias answered, "The head of John the Baptist."

And she came quickly to the king saying, "I will that you give to me on a charger the head of John the Baptist."

The king was exceedingly sorry, yet for his oath's sake and for their sakes which sat with him, he would not reject her.

And immediately the king sent an executioner, and commanded his head to be brought. And he went and beheaded John in prison. And brought his head on a charger, and gave it to the damsel. And the damsel gave it to her mother.

And when his disciples heard of it, they came and took his corpse, and laid it in a tomb.

Jesus departed by ship and when the people heard about it, they followed him on foot out of the cities.

When Jesus saw the great multitude he sorrowed, and healed their sick.

When it was evening his disciples came to him, "This is a deserted place, and the time is late. Send the people away, that they may go into the villages, and buy food for themselves."

But Jesus said, "They do not need to leave, give them some food."

"We only have five loaves of bread and two fish."

"Bring them to me."

Benjamin said, "But Master, we would not be able to feed this many disciples with five loaves of bread and two fish. There must be another alternative." And he scowled.

Jesus told everyone to sit on the grass. He took the five loaves and two fish and looking up to heaven, he blessed and broke them and gave them to his disciples to give to the multitude.

And everyone had all they could eat, and they retrieved the baskets and to their amazement they had twelve basket full left over.

Benjamin could not believe his eyes. He knew there were only five loaves of bread and two fish. How was he able to produce enough to feed this whole congregation?

And the ones who ate were about five thousand besides women and children.

Benjamin shook his head in unbelief. There did not seem to be anything he could not do. (I did not realize, when I met up with him on the road to Jerusalem that he was the Messiah. He did not tell me. Most of all I learned by what he did and his example. There could not be any other explanation. HE IS THE MESSIAH, THE ONLY BEGOTTEN OF THE FATHER. And he is *my* friend.) Benjamin beamed.

Again, they walked to a ship, and Jesus told his disciples to get into the boat and go to the other side to Bethsaida, while he said good bye to the multitude that had finished eating.

When they had gone, he went into a mountain to pray. When the disciples had gone about halfway and Jesus was by himself on the shore.

He noticed that they were having a hard time rowing because a strong wind was blowing. He went to them, walking on the sea.

They had figured it was a spirit, and called out and would have passed by them. They were terrified.

He immediately spoke to them saying, "It is I, do not be afraid." And he went to them in the ship. And the wind ceased.

They were extremely amazed.

Benjamin stared at Jesus and thought, (No one should be able to walk on the water. I would not even try. Only the Savior of the world would even attempt such a feat.)

When they had passed over to the other side, they came into the land of Gennesaret, and landed on the shore.

Jesus was tired. Everywhere he was seen, people came and brought others in droves, so he would heal them.

And when he entered the villages, cities or countries, they laid the sick in the streets, and begged him that they might touch the border of his clothes. And as many as touched his garment were healed.

Benjamin thought, (It is wonderful that because of the faith of the people, everyone would be healed of all ailments. Who knew that this would take place anywhere we, or I should say he, appears?)

———

Death of John the Baptist is found in the New Testament Mark 6:14-29

Jesus Heals An Invalid At Bethesda is found in the New Testament John 5:1-15

Jesus Feeds The 5000, Plus Women And Children is found in the New Testament Matthew 14:13-21

Jesus Walks On Water is found in the New Testament Mark 6:45-52

Jesus Heals Many In Gennesaret As They Touched His Garment is found in the New Testament Mark 6:53-56

Sickness Everywhere

As Jesus and his disciples were walking through the countryside, he decided to rest awhile.

One of his followers ran up to him and announced that there was an epidemic going through one of the near-by cities.

Jesus was still tired, but decided he had better go and see for himself.

"Please, everyone stay here and rest. If it is truly an epidemic, I do not want any of you to get ill. I will be back as soon as I am able. I am sure I will have a lot to do."

He asked the man who brought the information, to show him the way.

They had to go a great distance. He asked, "Do you know what the ailment is?"

"No, but they have red spots on their bodies and they itch. They have been told not to scratch, but that is hard when they itch all over."

"How have you kept from contracting the disease?" Jesus enquired.

"I have not been near anyone who has it. I was stopped outside of the city and was told not to enter and to go and find you", the man answered.

When he reached the city, he instructed the man not to enter with him, "Go back and tell my followers not to come to me. I am sure I will be busy for a while."

He did not know that Benjamin had been close behind him through his whole trek.

Benjamin caught up to his Master and entered the city right behind him.

A man was at the gate to greet Jesus and show him where he should start. He asked, "Who is the man behind you?"

Jesus turned to find Benjamin right on his heels.

"Why have you come? Now you will have to be quarantined."

"Will you have to be quarantined too?" Benjamin asked.

"No, I will not get the disease", Jesus answered.

"Then I will not either. I will go where you go. If you do not get the disease, then I will not," Benjamin stated emphatically.

"Benjamin, you do not know what you are saying. This disease could be and probably will be dangerous. Diseases like this are nothing to fool around with", Jesus said almost tearfully.

"But Jesus, if you are immune, why would I not be?"

Jesus just looked at him sympathetically. "Benjamin, please do not follow me around."

"You do not understand my feelings. I want to be able to help you in any way I can. I know I can be of help to you and all the citizens of this city."

"Well, it is too late now anyway. You have already been infected."

Jesus looked to the one who greeted them at the gate. "Please take Benjamin to a place that might be safe for him. He is a good friend of mine."

"Follow me," the man said to Benjamin.

"No, I am sorry, but I will stay with Jesus," Benjamin said dubiously.

The Master pointed for his friend to follow the gentleman.

"I have never disobeyed any of your commandments, but this time I must. I will not let you go into danger without me," answered Benjamin.

"Someday, I will be taken to a place where you cannot go and I will not return," Speaking of his death and resurrection.

Benjamin scratched his head. "Where will you go that I cannot go with you, where you will not return?"

Jesus said, "Show me to one of the diseased."

The gentleman guided the two visitors to a house. As they entered, they beheld a young girl of about eight years of age. She was thrashing around on her bed and moaned.

Jesus felt of her head. She seemed to be burning with a fever. Her body was covered with red spots that looked festered.

Jesus laid his hands on her head and commanded the disease to leave her body.

Immediately, the spots were gone as was the fever. She arose and got to her hands and knees and kissed the feet of Jesus, then asked, "Will you please heal my mother and father? Also, my brother lay over in the other bed."

Jesus turned around and looked at the boy of about three years of age. His face was shallow and sullen. It was obvious to the Master that he was dead.

Jesus went to the boy and put his hands in his and lifted him up. He said to him, "Arise and walk to your sister."

Immediately, the brother opened his eyes and smiled and arose and went and stood next to his sister. They hugged each other tightly.

Next, they both ran to Jesus and kissed both of his hands and thanked him.

Then he went to the parents and announced to them that their children were well. However, the parents were not. They had the disease also. Jesus went to them and prayed to his Father to be able to heal all he came in contact with.

"I will lay my hands on your heads and you will be healed." He did so and the parents were healed.

Benjamin followed Jesus everywhere he went. He loved watching the Master at his work. He wished he could do the same, so he could heal people, young and old, also. He had yet to learn his calling.

Jesus went throughout the city healing those who were ill. That was most of the people.

One day, when the two of them were going about making their rounds, Benjamin said, "I am not feeling very good. I feel sick to my stomach, and I have a terrible headache."

"Benjamin, I asked you to stay away. Now I fear you have the disease also."

"No, Sir, I am just tired. We have been working hard to keep the people well and functioning like they would like to. I will be alright. Let us continue until we have healed them all."

"Benjamin, I am worried about you. Your face is flushed and I think you have a fever. Stick out your tongue."

He did and it was abnormally red. He was starting to get red spots all over his body.

Jesus asked the people, who had been healed that were following him everywhere he and Benjamin went, "Would you have a place for my friend to lie down? I am afraid he has contracted the disease. He needs to rest."

One woman said, "My family is disease free and I have washed all of the bedding. He is welcome to stay with us. I have been watching you and I think I am able to take care of him."

Jesus answered, "You are too kind. Please take him and care for him while I am tending for others."

Benjamin was not happy about that, but he was getting too weak to argue. Now he knew why Jesus did not want him to come with him. He was starting to feel awful.

He followed the woman to her house and put him in a bed and covered him with blankets until he was warm enough.

Jesus would keep busy healing all of the townspeople and he did not have time to keep an eye on Benjamin. Besides he knew that the woman would take good care of him.

About a week had gone by and he was near the house Benjamin had been taken. He decided to look in on him.

When the woman saw Jesus coming to the house, she said, "He is not doing any better. Come see."

He walked into the bedroom, and Benjamin was thrashing back and forth, and the bed was soaked with sweat.

Jesus asked, "Have you given him any water to drink?"

She answered, "No, he said he did not want any. I could not get him to drink."

"Bring some water for him."

She complied.

Jesus took the cup of water and held Benjamin's head and dropped a little bit at a time into his mouth.

He drank it as fast as Jesus would put the drops in.

He opened his eyes, "Master you have come. Now I know that I will be healed."

"Yes, your faith will heal you."

With that, Benjamin sat up and proceeded to arise, but Jesus said, "Sit. Woman get him some broth to drink, so he can get his strength back."

"Yes, Sir". Then she went and brought some broth to him.

As the days went by and he got stronger, Benjamin was again in a hurry to be with his friend again.

By this time, Jesus had been through the whole town healing the populous. It was time to return to the apostles and other disciples to continue healing others. The town was now clean of any disease. He had also healed any who were lame, blind, disabled and any other maladies they may have.

He was very much loved by the whole country round about.

As the apostles and the others saw Jesus and Benjamin coming, they all ran up to them and violently hugged them and shook hands with both of them. Even Benjamin. Most of the time they thought he was a nuisance with all of his questions.

Benjamin had to tell them all about the diseases that Jesus healed. And how he had gotten it and also had to be healed by the only one who could.

A lot of the people hung around him. He had to tell the story over and over. But somehow he did not mind. Normally, no one wanted to be near him because of his questions. His popularity seemed to explode.

Jesus just looked on and smiled.

It was time to walk again and, of course, he had hundreds of followers. When they stopped, many more would join the throng.

Jesus would commence to preach to the congregation about things of God and His kingdom. Most loved to hear the new things he was teaching, but there were some who found the teachings too hard to understand and went their way.

When they started walking again, the extra people would be on their way to take care of their duties elsewhere.

They went again to the Sea of Galilee. They brought to him a man that was deaf and had a speech impediment; and they begged him to put his hand on him.

And he took him aside from the multitude, and put his fingers into his ears, and he spit and touched his tongue. And looking up to heaven, he sighed, and said to him be opened.

And immediately his ears were opened, and the string of his tongue was loosed, and he spoke plain.

He told them that they should tell no man; but the more he told them not to say anything to anyone; the more they published it. And they were so astonished that they said, "He has done all things well. He made both the deaf to hear and the dumb to speak.

They went again to the Sea of Galilee.

Jesus called his disciples and said to them. "I feel sorry for the multitude of people because they have been with me three days, and have nothing to eat. And if I send them away hungry to their own houses, they will faint by the way: for some of them have come a long way.

And his disciples answered him, "Where can a man satisfy these men with bread here in the wilderness?"

Jesus asked them, "How many loaves of bread do you have?"

And they said, "Seven".

And he told the people to sit down on the ground: and he took the seven loaves, and gave thanks, and broke the bread in pieces, and gave it to his disciples to set before them; and they did set them before the people.

And they had a few small fishes and he blessed, and commanded to set the fishes before them.

So they did eat, and were filled.

And they took up what had not been eaten and there were seven full baskets left.

And they who had eaten were about four thousand, then he sent them away.

———

The story of the Pox, I made up completely. Although it is entirely fiction, I thought it made a good story. Sometimes my imagination gets the best of me.

Jesus Heals The Deaf and Dumb Man is found in the New Testament Mark 7:31-37

Jesus feeds the 4000 plus women and children is found in the New Testament Mark 8:1-9

CHAPTER ELEVEN

More Miracles

Benjamin is so proud to be one of Jesus' good friends. He would do anything for him. ANYTHING!

What a great man he is. He is always thinking of the other people rather than himself. He even cares for animals. (I remember when we first came to Jerusalem. The little animals loved him so much; they followed him as long as they felt comfortable doing so. I realized then, that he was special. I did not realize at that time that he was the Messiah, Master of the world, Savior of the world, the Everlasting Father, the Prince of Peace.)

(I should have realized when we went into the city where everyone was sick with the Pox, that Jesus really could not get the disease, but I could. He tried so hard to dissuade me to stay away from the sick people, but because he could not get the Pox, I figured I too would be immune.

I got really sick. I had to be in bed for about two weeks before Jesus had time to help me. I thought I was going to die and wished I could. I had not been so miserable in all my life. I had the red spots that itched so bad, I thought I would go crazy. I was hot, but could not get warm. I know that does not make sense, but that was part of the malady. Then on top of all that, I did not feel like eating or drinking anything. Finally, Jesus was able to help me. Once he came to me, it was only minutes until I felt so much better, I was able to sip on a small amount of water and drink some broth to help me get my strength back. He is truly a miracle worker. On top of all that, he is the only begotten of the Father in the flesh. I do not know what I would do without him. And I do not want to find out.)

Soon Jesus, Benjamin, the twelve, and all of the rest of his followers were coming to Bethsaida, and they brought to him a blind man, and they asked him to touch him.

He took the blind man by the hand, and led him out of town; and when he had spit on his eyes, and put his hands on him, he asked the man if he could see anything.

The man looked up, and said, "I see men as trees, walking."

After that, he put his hands on his eyes again, and made him look up; and he was restored, and saw every man clearly.

And Jesus sent him away to his house saying, "Neither go into the town, nor tell it to anyone in the town.

Benjamin just marveled. He did not understand why Jesus would not want recognition for the deeds he had done. He deserved all the praise he was due.

Then he and his disciples went to the towns of Caesarea Philippi; and by the way he asked his disciples, saying, "Whom do men say that I am?"

And they answered, "John the Baptist, but some say, Elias, and others, one of the prophets."

But he said to them, "Whom do you say I am?"

And Peter answered and said, "You are the Christ."

And Jesus again said, "Tell no man who I am."

Benjamin was again confused. Why would the Master not want others to know who he is? We all know.

And Jesus began to teach them, "The Son of man must suffer many things, and be rejected of the elders, and of the chief priests, and scribes, and be killed, and after three days rise again."

And Peter took him and began to rebuke him.

But when he had turned around and looked on his disciples, he rebuked Peter, saying, "Get behind me Satan: for you do not think on the things of God, but you remember the things of men."

Jesus and his followers were walking when he saw a blind man who had been blind from his birth.

And his disciples asked him, "Master, who did sin, this man or his parents, which caused him to be born blind?"

Jesus answered, "Neither has this man sinned, nor his parents. The works of God should be shown in him. I must work the works of him that sent me. As long as I am in the world, I am the light of the world."

Benjamin thought, (Hmmm? I do not understand. Maybe if I listen more, the explanation will be made known to me.)

When Jesus had spoken, he spat on the ground and made clay of the spittle. And he put the clay on the eyes of the blind man.

And he said to him, "Go, wash in the pool of Siloam."

He went and washed, was able to see.

The neighbors, which knew that he was blind said, "Is this the man who sat and begged?"

Some said, "Yes, it is he." Others said, "It looks like him."

But he confessed, "I am the one."

So they asked him, "How were your eyes opened?"

He answered and said, "A man that is called Jesus made clay, and put it on my eyes, and then said, Go to the pool Siloam and wash, and I received my sight."

"Where is he?" they asked.

"I do not know", he said.

They brought the Pharisees to him that had been blind. It was the Sabbath when Jesus had made the man to see.

Then the Pharisees also asked him how he had received his sight. And he said, "He put clay on my eyes, and I washed and I can see."

Then said some of the Pharisees, "This man is not a man of God, because he does not keep the Sabbath day."

Others said, "How can a man who is a sinner do such miracles?"

And there was a division among them.

They asked the blind man again, "What do you think of the man that opened your eyes?"

He said, "He is a prophet."

But the Jews did not believe him. So they called his parents. And they asked them, saying, "Is this your son, who you say was born blind? How does he now see?"

"By what means he now sees, we do not know, or who opened his eyes, we do not know. He is of age, ask him. He can speak for himself."

Then they called the man that was blind again and said, "Give God the praise; we know that this man is a sinner."

He answered and said, "Whether he is a sinner or not, I do not know. One thing I *do* know, that, I was blind, and now I can see."

Then they said to him again, "What did he do to you? How did he open your eyes?"

He answered and said, "I have already told you and you would not hear. Do you think you would hear it again?"

Then the man continued, "Here is this marvelous thing and you do not know who he is? If this man were not of God, he could do nothing."

And Jesus sat for a while, contemplating what his father would have him teach, that he had not already conveyed to everyone.

The scribes started questioning him.

When all the people saw him, they ran to him and started praising him.

One of the multitude said, "Master, I have brought to you my son, which has a dumb spirit. And wherever he goes he foams at the mouth and gnashes with his teeth. And I spoke to your disciples and I said they should cast the dumb spirit out, and they would not do it.

He answered him, and said, "Oh faithless generation, how long will I be with you? How long will I be able to do the work for you? Bring him to me."

When Jesus saw him, he fell on the ground and started wallowing and foaming.

And he asked the boys father, "How long is it since he started doing this?"

And he said, "Since he was a child. And often it has cast him into the fire, and into water, to destroy him. But if you can do anything, have compassion on us, and help us."

Jesus said, "If you can believe, all things are possible."

Then the father of the child cried out in tears, "Lord, I believe; help my doubt."

When he saw the people running toward him, he said, "Dumb and deaf spirit, come out of him and never enter in him again."

And the spirit yelled and came out of him. And the child looked like he was dead. Many said that he was dead.

Jesus took him by the hand, and lifted him up.

When he had come to his disciples, they asked him privately, "Why were we not able to cast the devil out?"

And he said to them, "This kind cannot come forth, but by prayer and fasting."

They left and went through Galilee quietly so that no one knew. For he taught his disciples, saying, "The Son of man is going to be delivered into the hands of men, and they will kill him. And after he is killed, he will rise the third day."

None of the disciples understood that saying, and were afraid to ask him.

Benjamin thought maybe he knew what it meant, but he did not want to think about that possibility. Besides, if anything were to happen to his friend, he would be there to prevent it.

Jesus decided to ask his disciples, when he came to Capernaum and was in a house, "What were you arguing about when we were on our way here?"

But they would not tell him because they would wonder which of them was the greatest in Jesus' eyes.

He sat down and then called the twelve to him, "If any man desire to be first, the same will be last of all, and servant of all."

He took a child and set him in the middle of them, and when he had taken him in his arms, he said to them, "Whosoever will receive one of these children in my name, will receive me. And whosoever receive me, receives not me, but him that sent me."

Benjamin thought to himself, (I know that I am first, because I am his best friend).

John answered Jesus saying, "Master, we saw one man casting out devils in your name, but he does not follow us. And we told him to stop because he does not follow us."

Jesus said, "Forbid him not for there is no man which will do a miracle in my name, that can speak evil of me, for he that is not against us is for us."

———

Jesus Heals a Blind Man at Bethsaida is found in the New Testament Mark 8:22-26

Jesus Heals Man Blind From Birth is found in the New Testament John 9:1-33

Jesus Heals Boy with Unclean Spirit is found in the New Testament Mark 9:14-29

CHAPTER
TWELVE

Miracles Continue

Benjamin loved being with Jesus all the time. He loved learning from him. He loved how His love was unconditional. "How could he love everyone the same? It did not matter if the person was good or evil. He loves them all. I have found it hard to love everyone the same. I will follow Him all of my life. I will contend with anyone who speaks evil against my Lord."

When they came to Capernaum, some men came to Peter expecting tribute money. They said to him, "Does your master not pay tribute?"

Peter said, "Yes".

When he came into the house, Jesus stopped him saying, "What are you thinking, Simon? Of whom do the kings of the earth take custom or tribute? Of their own children or strangers?"

Peter said to him, "Of strangers."

Jesus said to him, "Then are the children free. However, so we do not offend them, go to the sea, and cast a hook, and take up the fish that is caught first, and when you open his mouth, you will find a piece of money. Take it and give it to them for you and me."

Benjamin thought, (Who ever heard of such a thing? A fish with money in its mouth. How did he know that the fish with the money in its mouth would be caught first? He is amazing.)

Jesus loved to teach in parables. One day he asked, "What do you think? If a man has a hundred sheep and one of them goes astray, does he not leave the ninety and nine, and go into the mountains, and look for the one that is lost? Even so it is not the will of your Father which is in heaven, that one of his little ones should perish."

Benjamin wanted to ask what that parable meant, but he was afraid that he would look like an idiot. I'm sure there will be other parables.

Jesus left Galilee and came into the coasts of Judea beyond Jordan. And the multitude followed him, and he healed them there.

The Pharisees also came to him tempting him and saying, "Is it lawful for a man to divorce his wife for any reason?"

And he answered and said to them, "Have you not read that he which made them in the beginning made them male and female. And said for this cause should a man leave father and mother and should cleave to his wife and they will be one flesh. Wherefore, they are no more two, but one flesh. What therefore God has joined together, let no man put asunder. In other words they should not be divided."

They said to him, "Why did Moses command to divorce a wife and put her away?"

He said to them, "Because of the hardness of your hearts you were told to divorce your wives, but from the beginning it was not so."

"And I say to you that whosoever should divorce his wife, except it be for fornication, and will marry another, he commits adultery."

Benjamin said, "I have never heard that before."

Jesus smiled at him and said, "There are many things to be learned while on this earth. Any knowledge you get while on this earth, you will take with you when you go to heaven."

"Well, then, I had better learn all I can. I will stay with you and remember what I am able."

Again, Jesus smiled.

Then was brought to him a man possessed with a devil, blind and dumb and he healed him, insomuch that the blind and dumb both spoke and saw.

And the people were amazed, and said, "Is this the son of David?"

But when the Pharisees heard it, they said, "This fellow only casts out devils by Beelzebub, the prince of the devils."

Jesus knew their thoughts and said, "If Satan cast out Satan, he is divided against himself. How then can his kingdom stand? And if I cast out devils by the Spirit of God, the kingdom of God will come to you. He that is not with me is against me, and he that is not with me is with Satan."

"Wherefore I say to you, all manner of sin and blasphemy will be forgiven, but blasphemy against the Holy Ghost will not be forgiven.

And whosoever speaks a word against the Son of man, it will be forgiven him, but whosoever speaks against the Holy Ghost, it will not be forgiven him, neither in this world, neither in the world to come."

On the Sabbath Jesus was teaching in one of the Synagogues. And there was a woman which had been crippled eighteen years and was bent over and could not lift herself up.

And when Jesus saw her, he called her to him, and said to her, "Woman, you are healed from your affliction."

And he laid his hand on her and immediately she was made straight, and she glorified God.

And the ruler of the Synagogue answered with indignation, because Jesus had healed on the Sabbath day, and said to the people, "There are six days in which men should work: in them therefore come and be healed, and not on the Sabbath day."

The Lord then answered him and said, "You hypocrite, do not each of you lose his ox or his ass from the stall, and lead him to water on the Sabbath? And this woman, who is a daughter of Abraham, whom Satan has bound these eighteen years, be healed from this bond on the Sabbath day?"

And when he had said these things, all of his adversaries were ashamed. And all the people rejoiced for all the glorious things that were done by him.

And he went through the cities and villages, teaching and journeying toward Jerusalem.

Then said Benjamin to him, "Lord, there are few that will be saved?"

And he said to them, "Try to enter in the straight gate, for many will seek to enter in, and will not be able. When once the master of the house has gotten up and shut the door, and you begin to stand outside, and knocked saying, "Lord, Lord, open the door for us."

And he will answer and say to you, "I do not know you. Who are you?"

Then will you begin to say, "We have eaten and drunk in your presence, and you have taught in our streets."

But he will say, "I tell you, I do not know who you are. Go away all you workers of iniquity."

"There will be weeping and gnashing of teeth, when you will see Abraham, and Isaac, and Jacob, and all the prophets, in the kingdom of God, and you have been thrown out."

As Jesus went into the house of one of the chief Pharisee to eat bread on the Sabbath day, they watched him.

And behold, there was a certain man before him which had the dropsy.

And Jesus spoke to the lawyers and Pharisees, saying, "Is it lawful to heal on the Sabbath day?"

And they could not answer him.

And he healed him, and let him go.

And Jesus also taught in parables.

And he said, "Which of you will have an ass or an ox that has fallen into a pit, and will not go and pull him out on the Sabbath day?"

Again they did not answer.

And he told another parable. "Those who were invited to a wedding, do not sit in the highest room, in case a more honorable man than you are invited. And he that invited you and him saying to you, "Give this man your place, and you being shamed go and sit down in the lowest room."

"But when you are invited, go and sit down in the lowest room, that when he that invited you comes, he may say, "Friend, go up higher. Then will you have worship in the presence of them that sit and eat with you."

"For whosoever exalts himself will be shamed, and he that humbles himself will be higher."

"When you make dinner or a supper, do not call your friends, nor your brethren, nor relatives, nor rich neighbors, because they will invite you to their meals that they may pay you back."

"But when you make a feast, call the poor, the maimed, the lame, and the blind, you will be blessed, for they cannot pay you back, for you will be paid back at the resurrection of the just."

Benjamin said, "It is more righteous to feed the poor and not expect anything in return, than to feed the rich who feel they must feed you in return."

Jesus looked at him and said, "You have learned many good things."

Then Jesus said to those who think they are of high rank, "A certain man made a great supper, and invited many."

"And he sent his servant at supper time to say to them that were invited, 'Come, for all things are now ready.'"

"And they all with one accord began to make excuse. The first said, 'I have bought a piece of ground, and I must needs go and see it. I pray you have me excused.'"

"And another said, 'I have bought five yoke of oxen, and I go to prove them. I pray you have me excused.'"

"And another said, 'I have married a wife, and therefore I cannot come.'"

"So that servant came and showed his lord these things. Then the master of the house being angry said to his servant, 'Go out quickly into the streets and lanes of the city, and bring in here the poor, and the maimed, and the lame, and the blind.'"

"And the servant said, 'Lord, it is done as you have commanded, and yet there is room'".

"And the lord said to the servant, 'Go out into the highways and pathways, and compel them to come in, that my house may be filled."

"For I say to you, That none of those men which were invited will taste of my supper."

———

Miraculous Temple Tax in a fish's mouth Is found in the New Testament Matthew 17:24-27

Jesus Heals a Blind, Mute Demoniac Is found in the New Testament Matthew12:22-33

Jesus Heals a Woman Who Had Been Crippled for 18 years is found in the New Testament Luke 13:10-17

Jesus Heals a Man with Dropsy on the Sabbath is found in the New Testament Luke 14:1-6

CHAPTER
THIRTEEN

Teaching in Jerusalem Again

Jesus loved to teach in parables. It gave his disciples something to think about and how it might apply to them.

Jesus said, "There was a certain rich man, which was clothed in purple and fine linen, and fared sumptuously every day."

"And there was a certain beggar named Lazarus, which was laid at his gate, full of sores. And he was hoping to be fed with the crumbs which fell from the rich man's table and the dogs came and licked his sores."

"And the beggar died, and was carried by the angels into Abraham's bosom. The rich man died also, and was buried."

"And in hell the rich man lifted his eyes, being in torment, and saw Abraham with Lazarus in his bosom."

"And the rich man cried and said, 'Father Abraham, have mercy on me, and send Lazarus, that he may dip the tip of his finger in water, and cool my tongue, for I am tormented in this flame.'"

"But Abraham said, 'Son remember that you in your lifetime received the good things, and Lazarus received evil things? But now he is comforted, and you are tormented.'"

"And because all this, between us and you there is a great gulf, so that they which would pass from here to you cannot, neither can they pass to us."

"Then he said, 'I pray, Father, that you would send him to my father's house, for I have five brothers, which may testify to them, so they will not also come to this place of torment.'"

"Abraham said to him, 'They have Moses and the prophets, let them hear them.'"

"And the rich man said, 'No, Father Abraham, but if one went to them from the dead, they will repent.'"

"And he said to him, 'If they would not hear Moses and the prophets, neither will they be persuaded, though one rose from the dead.'"

Benjamin said, "I would rather be with Father Abraham than to look from the abyss and wish I had a little water."

"Yes", Jesus remarked, "Always look to be the best you can be, so that you will not be in torment after this life."

"Listen, if you find fault with your brother, go and tell him his fault between you and him alone. If he will hear you, you will have gained a brother."

"But if he will not hear you, take with you one or two more, that in the mouth of two or three witnesses every word will be established."

"And if he will neglect to hear them, tell it to the church, but if he neglect to hear the church, let him be to you as a heathen."

When Jesus and his disciples entered a certain village, there were ten men standing a ways off and they were lepers.

They said to him, "Jesus, Master, have mercy on us."

And when he saw them, he said, "Go show yourselves to the priests." As they went, they were cleansed.

And one of them, when he saw that he was healed, turned back and with a loud voice glorified God, and fell down at Jesus' feet, giving him thanks, and he was a Samaritan.

And Jesus said, "Were there not ten that were cleansed? But where are the nine?"

"There were not any that returned to give glory to God, except this stranger.

"Arise and go your way, your faith has made you whole."

Now a certain man was sick, named Lazarus, of Bethany, the town of Mary and Martha his sisters.

They sent for Jesus saying, "Lord behold, he whom you love is sick."

When Jesus heard this he said, "This sickness will not cause his death."

Now Jesus loved Martha, and her sister, and Lazarus.

When he heard that he was sick, he stayed two days in the same place where he was.

Then he said to his disciples, "Let us go to Judea again."

His disciples said to him, "Master, the Jews seek to stone you, and you want to go there again?"

"Our friend, Lazarus is sleeping, but I go that I might awake him out of sleep."

Then his disciples said, "Lord, if he sleeps, he will be alright."

However, Jesus spoke of his death: but they thought that he had spoken of resting in sleep.

Then Jesus spoke to them plainly, "Lazarus is dead."

Then when Jesus came, he found that he had lain in the grave four days already.

Many of the Jews came to Martha and Mary, to comfort them concerning their brother.

Then Martha, as soon as she heard that Jesus was coming, went and met him, but Mary sat still in the house.

Then Martha said to Jesus, "Lord, if you had been here, my brother would not have died. But I know, that even now, whatsoever you will ask of God, God will give it to you."

Jesus said to her, "Your brother shall rise again."

Martha said to him, "I know that he will rise again in the resurrection at the last day."

Jesus said to her, "I am the resurrection, and the life. He that believes in me, though he were dead, yet will he live. And whosoever lives and believes in me will never die. Do you believe this?"

She said, "Yes, Lord, I believe that you are the Christ, the Son of God, which will come into the world."

And when she had said this, she went to the house, and called Mary her sister secretly, saying, "The Master is here and is calling for you."

As soon as she heard that, she arose quickly and came to him.

Now Jesus was not yet come into the town, but was in that place where Martha met him.

The Jews then which were with her in the house, and comforted her, when they saw Mary, that she got up in a hurry and went out, followed her saying, "She is going to the grave to weep."

Then when Mary had come where Jesus was, and saw him, she fell down at his feet, saying, "Lord, if you had been here, my brother would not have died."

When Jesus saw her crying, and the Jews also crying which came with her, he groaned, and he was troubled, and said, "Where have you laid him?"

They said, "Lord, come and see."

Jesus wept.

Then the Jews said, "Look how he loved him!"

And some of them said, "This man, which opened the eyes of the blind, could he have prevented this man from dying?"

Jesus, again groaning came to the grave. It was a cave, and a stone lay on it.

Jesus said, "Take away the stone."

Martha said, "Lord, by this time he stinks, for he has been dead four days."

Jesus said to her, "Did not I tell you, if you would believe, you should see the glory of God?"

Then they took the stone away from the sepulcher.

And Jesus lifted his eyes, and said, "Father, I thank you that you have heard me. And I know that you hear me always, but because of the people which stand by, I said it, that they may believe that you have sent me."

And when he had said these things, he cried with a loud voice, Lazarus come here."

And Lazarus came forth, bound hand and foot with grave clothes, and his face was bound with a napkin.

Jesus said to them, "Loose him."

And they let him go.

Then many of the Jews which came to Mary, and had seen the things that Jesus had done, believed in him.

But some of them went to the Pharisees and told them what Jesus had done.

Then the chief priests and the Pharisees gathered in a council, and said, "What should we do? He does many miracles.

Then from that day, they took counsel to put him to death!

And the Passover was soon and many went out of the country up to Jerusalem to purify themselves.

Then they watched for Jesus, and spoke among themselves, as they stood in the temple, "Do you think that he will come to the feast?"

Now both the chief priests and the Pharisees had given a commandment, that if any man knew where he was, he should show it, that they might take him.

———

Parable of the Rich Man and the Beggar is found in the New Testament Luke 16:19-31

Teaching of Fault between Brothers is found in the New Testament Matthew 18:15-17

Jesus raises Lazarus from the Dead in Bethany is found in the New Testament John 11:1-45

Authorities Seek to kill Jesus is found in the New Testament John 11:55-57

CHAPTER
FOURTEEN

Passover

When Jesus and his disciples came close to Jerusalem he sent two of his disciples, including Benjamin, saying, "Go into the village and you will find an ass tied, and a colt with her. Loose them, and bring them to me."

"And if any man says anything to you, then say, 'The Lord has need of them.' And he will send them."

All this was done to fulfill which was spoken by the prophet saying, "Tell the daughter of Sion, 'Behold, your King comes to you, meek, and sitting on an ass, and a colt the foal of an ass.'"

And the disciples went, and did as Jesus commanded them. And brought the ass, and the colt, and put on them their clothes. And they set him on it.

And a very great multitude spread their garments in the way. Others cut down branches from the trees, and laid them in the way.

And the multitudes that went before, and that followed, cried saying, "Hosanna to the Son of David. Blessed is he that comes in the name of the Lord. Hosanna in the highest."

And when he came into Jerusalem, everyone wondered, "Who is this?"

And the multitude said, "This is Jesus the prophet of Nazareth of Galilee."

And Jesus went into the temple of God, and cast out all them that sold and bought in the temple, and overthrew the tables of money changers, and the seats of them that sold doves.

And he said to them, "It is written, MY house will be called the house of prayer, but you have made it a den of thieves."

And the blind and the lame came to him in the temple, and he healed them.

And when the chief scribes and priests saw the wonderful things that he did, and the children crying in the temple and saying, "Hosanna to the Son of David," they were not happy.

And they said to him, "Do you hear what they say?"

And Jesus said to them, "Yes, have you never read, 'Out of the mouth of babes and sucklings you have perfected praise".

In the morning he was hungry. He saw a fig tree while he was walking. When he examined the tree, there was nothing on it. It only had leaves. And he said to the tree, "Let no fruit grow on these forever."

And right away the fig tree withered and died.

And when the disciples saw it, they were amazed, and Benjamin said, "It was quick that the fig tree withered.

Jesus answered and said to them, "If you have faith and doubt not, you will not only do this, which was done to the fig tree, but also you can say to this mountain, 'Be removed and cast in the sea, it will be done."

"And all things you ask in prayer, believing, you will receive."

It was getting time for the Passover and his disciples came to him and asked, "Where should we prepare for you to eat the Passover?"

And Jesus said, "Go into the city to such a man, and say to him, "The Master said, 'MY time is at hand. I will keep the Passover at your house with my disciples.'"

Benjamin went looking for the place that the Passover should be kept. He could not find a place he thought was suitable.

And the disciples did as Jesus told them. And they made the place ready for the celebration.

Now when it was evening, he sat down with the twelve.

Benjamin still was not found. He was still looking for just the right place.

As Jesus and the twelve ate, he said, "One of you will betray me this night."

Each one asked, "Lord is it I?"

And he answered and said, "He that dips his hand with me in the dish, the same will betray me."

"The Son of man goes as it is written of him, but woe to that man by whom the Son of man is betrayed. It had been good for that man if he had not been born.

Then Judas, which betrayed him, answered and said, "Master is it I?

And Jesus said to him, "You said it."

As they were eating, Jesus took bread, and blessed it, and broke it into pieces. And gave it to his disciples, and said, "Take, eat, this is my body."

And he took the cup, and gave thanks, and gave it to them saying, "Drink all of it. For this is my blood of the new testament, which is shed for many for the remission of sins."

"But I say to you, I will not drink of this fruit of the vine, until that day when I drink it new with you in my Father's kingdom."

Jesus arose from supper, and laid aside his garments, and took a towel, and put it around him.

Then he poured water in a bowl and began to wash the disciples' feet, and to wipe them with the towel he had around him.

When he came to Simon Peter, and Peter said to him, "Lord, will you wash my feet?"

Jesus answered and said to him, "What I do you know not now, but you will know hereafter."

Peter said, "You will never wash my feet."

Jesus answered him, "If I do not wash you, you have no part with me."

Simon Peter said to him, "Lord, not only my feet, but also my hands and my head."

Jesus said to him, "He that is washed does not need to wash his feet, but is clean all over, but not all."

For he knew who should betray him. Therefore he said, "You are not all clean."

So after he had washed their feet, and had taken his garments, and was set down again, he said to them, "Know what I have done to you?"

"You call me Master and Lord, and you are right. For I am."

"If then, your feet, you also should wash one another's feet. For I have given you an example. That you should do as I have done to you."

When Jesus said, "One of you will betray me."

Then the disciples looked one on another, doubting of whom he spoke.

Now there was one of his disciples, whom Jesus loved, leaning on his bosom.

Simon Peter asked of him, that he should ask who it could be that he spoke of.

He then lying on Jesus' breast said to him, "Lord who is it?"

"He it is to whom I give bread to dip, when I have dipped it."

And when he had dipped it, he gave it to Judas Iscariot.

Then after, Satan entered into Judas.

Then said Jesus to him, "What you are going to do, do quickly."

Now no man at the table knew what Jesus meant when he spoke to Judas.

For some of them thought, because Judas had the bag, that Jesus wanted him to buy those things that we have need for the feast. Or that he should give something to the poor.

Then Judas went right out, and it was night.

———

Jesus cleanses the Temple is found in the New Testament Matthew 21:12-16

Preparations for the Passover is found in the New Testament Matthew 21:17-29

Jesus Washing Disciples Feet is found in the New Testament John 13:4-15

Jesus Sent Judas Iscariot out is found in the New Testament John 13:18-30

CHAPTER
FIFTEEN

Jesus' Death

"A new commandment I give to you, that you love one another as I have loved you. That you also love one another. By this will men know that you are my disciples, if you have love one for another.

Simon Peter said, "Lord, where are you going?"

Jesus answered him, "Where I go, you cannot follow me now. But you will follow me later.

Peter said to him, "Lord, why can I not follow you now? I will lay down my life for your sake."

Jesus answered him, "Will you lay down your life for my sake? I say to you, the cock will not crow, till you have denied me three times."

"Let not your heart be troubled. You believe in God, believe in me also."

"In my Father's house are many mansions. If it were not so, I would have told you. I go to prepare a place for you. And if I go and prepare a place for you, I will come again, and receive you to myself, that where I am, there you may be also. And where I go you know, and you know the way."

Thomas said, "Lord, we do not know where you are going, and how can we know the way?"

Jesus said to him, "I am the way, the truth, and the life. No man comes to the Father, but by me."

"If you had known me, you should have known my Father also. And from now on you know him, and have seen him."

Philip said, "Lord, show us the Father, and we will be satisfied."

Jesus said to him, "Have I been so long time with you, and yet you have not known me, Philip? He that has seen me has seen the Father. And how can you say to them, Show us the Father?"

"Do you believe that I am in the Father, and the Father in me? The words that I speak to you I speak not of myself. But the Father that dwells in me, he does the work."

"He that believes in me, the works that I do will he do also. And greater works than these will he do, because I go to my Father. And whosoever will ask in my name, that will I do, that the Father may be glorified in the Son."

"If you will ask any thing in my name, I will do it."

"Peace I leave with you, my peace I give unto you, not as the world give I unto you. Let not your heart be troubled, neither let it be afraid."

"We need to go now."

When they were outside, they came upon Benjamin.

Jesus said, "Where have you been? You missed the feast of the Passover."

"I was looking for a place to have the Passover." He put his head in his hands and wept bitterly. "How could I have missed the Passover?"

"Lord, forgive me."

But would he ever be able to forgive himself.

"Men will put you out of Synagogues, and the time will come that whosoever will kill you will think that he does God's service. And they will do these things to you because they have not known the Father nor me."

"But now I go my way to him that sent me. But because I have said these things to you, sorrow has filled your heart."

"A little while, and you will not see me and again, a little while, and you will see me, because I go to the Father."

Then said some of the disciples among themselves, "What is this that he said to us, 'A little while, and you will not see me. And again, a little while, and you will see me. And, because I go to the Father?'"

They said therefore, "What is this that he says, 'A little while? We cannot tell what he says.'"

"A woman when she is in travail feels sorrow, because her hour has come, but as soon as she is delivered of the child, she remembers the pain no more, for joy that a child is born into the world."

"And you now have sorrow, but I will see you again, and your heart will rejoice, and your joy no man can take away."

"Behold, the hour now comes, that you will be scattered, every man to his own, and will leave me alone. And yet I am not alone, because the Father is with me."

"These things I have spoken to you, that in me you might have peace. In the world you will have tribulation, but be happy, I have overcome the world."

These words Jesus spoke, and lifted his eyes up to heaven, and said, "Father, the hour has come. Glorify your Son, that Your Son also may glorify you. As you have given him power over all flesh, that he will give eternal life to as many as you have given him."

"And this is life eternal, that they might know you the only true God, and Jesus Christ, whom you have sent. I have glorified you on the earth. I have finished the work which you gave me to do."

"And now, O Father, glorify me with your own self, with the glory which I had with you before the world was. I have manifested your name to the men which you have given me out of the world."

"Yours they were, and you gave them to me, and they have kept your word. Now they have known that all things whatsoever you have given me are from you. For I have given to them the words which you gave me. And they have received them, and have known surely that I came out from you, and they have believed that you did send me."

"I pray for them. I pray not for the world, but for them which you have given me, for they are yours. And all mine are yours, and I am glorified in them. And now I am no more in the world, but these are in the world, and I come to you."

"Holy Father, keep through your own name those whom you have given me that they may be one, as we are."

"While I was with them in the world, I kept them in your name. Those that you gave to me I have kept, and none of them is lost, but the son of perdition, that the scripture might be fulfilled."

"And now I come to you, and these things I speak in the world that they might have my joy fulfilled in them."

"I have given them your word, and the world has hated them, because they are not of the world, even as I am not of the world."

"I pray not that you should take them out of the world, but that you should keep them from the evil."

"They are not of the world, even as I am not of the world."

"Sanctify them through your truth. Your word is truth."

"As you have sent me into the world, even so have I also sent them into the world."

"And for their sakes I sanctify myself, that they also might be sanctified through the truth."

"Neither pray I for these alone, but for them also which will believe on me through their word."

"That they may all be one, as you, Father, are in me, and I in you, that they also may be one in us. That the world may believe that you have sent me."

And the glory which you gave to me I have given them, that they may be one, even as we are one."

"I in them, and you in me. That they may be made perfect in one in me; and that the world may know that you sent me, and has loved them, as you have loved me."

"Father, I will that they also, that you have given me, be with me where I am; that they may behold my glory, which you have given me. For you loved me before the foundation of the world."

"O righteous Father, the world has not known you, but I have known you, and those have known that you love me."

"And I have declared to them your name, and will declare it. That the love wherewith you have loved me may be in them, and I in them."

After Jesus had spoken these words, he went with his disciples over the brook Cedron, where there was a garden, into which he and his disciples entered. And Judas also which betrayed him, he knew the place, for Jesus often came here with his disciples.

Benjamin stated to one of the other disciples, "He gave such a beautiful prayer to his Father. What more can he say?"

The other disciple just looked at him and said nothing. There was nothing he *could* say.

Judas then, having with him a band of men and officers from the chief priests and Pharisees. They came with lanterns, and torches and weapons.

Jesus knowing all, went and said to them, "Who are you looking for?"

They answered, "Jesus of Nazareth."

Jesus said, "I am he."

Then he said again, "Who are you looking for?"

And they said, "Jesus of Nazareth."

Jesus answered, "I have told you that I am he. If I am the one you want, let these go their way."

That the saying might be fulfilled, which he spoke, "Of them which you gave to me, I have not lost any."

Then Simon Peter having a sword drew it, and cut off the ear of the high priests servant. The servant's name was Malchus.

Then Jesus said to Peter, "Put your sword in the sheath. The cup which my Father has given me, should I not drink it?"

Jesus touched his ear, and healed him.

Then the band took Jesus and bound him. And led him to Annas first, for he was the father-in-law to Caiaphas, which was the high priest that same year.

Now Caiaphas was he, which gave counsel to the Jews that it was expedient that one man should die for the people.

Simon Peter followed Jesus, and so did Benjamin. Benjamin went in with Jesus. And he spoke to her that kept the door, and brought in Peter.

Then said the girl that kept the door to Peter, "Are you also one of this man's disciples?"

He said, "I am not."

And the servants and officers stood there, who had made a fire of coals; for it was cold, and they warmed themselves. And Peter stood with them and warmed himself.

The high priest then asked Jesus of his disciples and of his doctrine.

Jesus answered him, "I spoke openly to the world. I even taught in the synagogue, and in the temple, where the Jews always stay. And in secret I have said nothing. Why ask me? Ask them who heard me, what I have said to them. They know what I said."

And when he had spoken, one of the officers which stood by struck Jesus with the palm of his hand, saying, "Answered you the high priest so?"

Jesus answered him, "If I have spoken evil, bear witness of the evil, but if well, why slap me?"

Now Annas had sent him bound to Caiaphas the high priest.

And Simon Peter stood and warmed himself. They said to him, "Are you one of his disciples?"

He denied it and said, "I am not."

One of the servants of the high priest, being related to the one whose ear was cut off said, "Did I see you in the garden with him?"

Peter again denied the fact that he was with Jesus in the garden with him, and immediately the cock crew.

Then Jesus was led from Caiaphas to the hall of judgment. And it was early.

Pilate then went out to them and said, "What is he accused of?"

He answered and said, "If he were not a malefactor, we would not have delivered him up at this time."

Then Pilate said, "Take him, and judge him according to your law."

The Jews said to him, "It is not lawful for us to put any man to death."

Then Pilate went in to the judgment hall again, and called Jesus, and said to him, "Are you the King of the Jews?"

Jesus answered him, "Do you say this by yourself, or did others tell you about me?"

Pilate asked, "Am I a Jew? Your own nation and the chief priests have delivered you to me. What have you done?"

Jesus answered, "My kingdom is not of this world. If my kingdom were of this world, then would my servants fight, that I should not be taken to the Jews, but now is my kingdom not from here."

Pilate said to him, "Are you a king then?"

Jesus answered, "You say I am a king. This was why I was born, and this is why I came into the world. That I should bear witness of the truth. Every one that is of the truth hears my voice."

Pilate asked, "What is truth?" And when he had said this, he went out again to the Jews, and say to them, "I do not find any fault in him at all."

But you have a custom, that I should release one at the Passover. Would you want me to release to you the King of the Jews?"

Then they all cried again saying, "Not this man, but Barabbas." Now Barabbas was a robber.

Benjamin was in the crowd and yelled, "Save Jesus, King of the Jews!"

Most of the people in the crowd wanted Barabbas freed and Jesus hung.

Benjamin sobbed. He had been with Jesus even before they came to Jerusalem. They could not kill him. He was born to be king.

The people threw rocks at Benjamin. They forced him out of Jerusalem.

Then Pilate took Jesus and scourged him. And the soldiers made a crown of thorns and placed it on his head. And they put a purple robe on him.

And they said, "Hail, King of the Jews."

And they slapped him with their hands.

Pilate went again before the people and said, "Behold, I bring him out to you, that you may know I find no fault in him."

Then Jesus came in front of the crowd wearing the crown of thorns, and the purple robe. And Pilate said, "Behold the man!"

When the chief priests and officers saw him, they cried out, saying, "Crucify him, crucify him."

Pilate said to them, "You take him, and crucify him, for I find no fault in him."

The Jews answered him, "We have a law, and by our law he should die, because he made himself the Son of God.'"

When Pilate heard that saying, he was more afraid.

And went again into the judgment hall, and said to Jesus, "Who are you?

But Jesus gave him no answer.

Then said Pilate to him, "You will not speak to me? Do you not know that I have power to crucify you, and have power to release you?"

Jesus answered, "You could have no power at all against me, except it were given to you from above. He that delivered me to you has the greater sin."

And from that time, Pilate wanted to release Jesus. But the Jews cried out, saying, "If you let this man go, you are not a friend of Caesar. Whosoever makes himself a king speaks against Caesar."

When Pilate heard that, he brought Jesus and sat down in the judgment seat. And Pilate brought Jesus forward and said to the Jews, "Behold your King."

But they cried out, "Away with him, away with him, crucify him."

Pilate said to them, "Should I crucify your King?"

The chief priests said, "We have no king but Caesar."

Then he delivered him to them to be crucified. And they took Jesus and led him away.

And he bearing his cross went to a place called the place of a skull, which is called in Hebrew Golgotha.

They crucified him, and two other with him, one on either side with Jesus in the middle.

And Pilate wrote a title, and put it on the cross. And the writing was, JESUS OF NAZARATH THE KING OF THE JEWS.

This title then read many of the Jews, for the place where Jesus was crucified was close to the city, and it was written in Hebrew, and Greek, and Latin.

Then the chief priests of the Jews said to Pilate, "Do not write, The King of the Jews, but that he said, I am King of the Jews."

Pilate answered, "What I have written I have written."

Then the soldiers, when they had crucified Jesus, took his garments, and made four parts, to every solder a part. And also his coat. Then they said among themselves, "Let us not do anything to the coat, but cast lots for it."

The scripture was fulfilled which stated, "They parted my garments among them, and for my robe they cast lots."

Now there stood by the cross of Jesus Benjamin, Jesus' mother, and his mother's sister, Mary the wife of Cleophas, and Mary Magdalene.

When Jesus saw his mother, and John standing by, he said to his mother, "Woman, behold your son!"

Then he said to John, "Behold your mother."

From that hour John took her to his home.

Benjamin stood off to the side and cried uncontrollably. It had started raining hard, so no one could see Benjamin's tears. Now he was alone. He had no one. Jesus was all that he had. Now he was gone to be with his Father. Then through his tears and rain, he smiled, "Sometime I too will go to be with our Father."

———

Jesus' Intercessory Prayer is found in the New Testament John 17:1-26

Peter Denies Knowing Jesus 3 Times is found in the New Testament John 18:17-18

Jesus Repairs Servants Ear is found in the New Testament Luke 22:50-51

Jesus' Trial is found in the New Testament John 19:1-14

CPSIA information can be obtained
at www.ICGtesting.com
Printed in the USA
BVHW081236301121
622781BV00007B/366